WI

Prayer of Saint Francis

Lord, make me an instrument
of your peace.
Where there is hatred, let
me sow love;
Where there is injury,
pardon;
Where there is doubt,
faith;
Where there is despair,
hope;
Where there is darkness,
light;
Where there is sadness,
joy;
O Divine Master, grant that
I may not so much seek to be
consoled as to console;
To be understood as to
understand;
To be loved as to love;
For it is in the giving that we
receive;
It is in the pardoning that we
are pardoned;
It is in the dying that we are
born to eternal life.

—Saint Francis of Assisi
1181-1226

Care Enough to Discipline

Raising Children for the 21st Century

Care Enough to Discipline

Raising Children for the 21st Century

*A Universal Guide for Parents and Educators
Who Really Care About Children Becoming
Successful Adults*

DR. LANE S. ANDERSON

www.ivyhousebooks.com

Because of the dynamic nature of the Internet, any web addresses or links contained in this book may have changed since publication and may no longer be valid.

All references to scripture are from *The Holy Bible*, King James Version.

PUBLISHED BY IVY HOUSE PUBLISHING GROUP
5122 Bur Oak Circle, Raleigh, NC 27612
United States of America
919-782-0281
www.ivyhousebooks.com

ISBN13: 978-1-57197-500-3
Library of Congress Control Number: 2009906747

Printed in the United States of America

*Dedicated to all children everywhere in our global family
and to "Charlie" for her courage,
compassion, intelligence, and beauty.
She will always be the love of my life.*

Note to the Reader

I wrote *Care Enough to Discipline* because of what is happening inside America today, especially with regard to our families and schools, which are the foundation for any society. Though we are the greatest nation on earth in terms of diversity and opportunity, we need to be unified in our collective purpose and positive universal values, which govern our actions, expectations, and dreams. Doing the right thing at the right time for the right reason is the essence of character of which discipline, respect, courage, and compassion are the chief components. If our country continues to decline in these worthy traits, we will lose our common resolve and collective will, as well as an innate sense of responsibility and accountability. This decline will destroy our country from the inside, which is ultimately a greater threat than occasional terrorist attacks or the potential for nuclear annihilation. *Care Enough to Discipline* is simply a guide on how critical discipline can be in the process of children being taught by the most important teachers in their early lives: parents and educators.

*I believe that friends and family are quiet angels who lift
us to our feet when our wings have trouble
remembering how to fly.*
—Anonymous

*A hundred years from now it will not matter what my bank account
was, the type of house I lived in, or the kind of car I drove—but the
world may be different beacuse I was
important in the life of a child.*
—Anonymous

*Suffer the little children to come unto me, and forbid them not:
for of such is the Kingdom of God.*
—Mark 10:14

TABLE OF CONTENTS

THE STARFISH STORY

There was a young man walking down a deserted beach just before dawn. In the distance he saw a frail old man. As he approached the old man, he saw him picking up stranded starfish and throwing them back into the sea. The young man gazed in wonder as the old man again and again threw the starfish from the sand to the water. He asked, "Old man, why do you spend so much energy doing what seems to be a waste of time?" The old man explained that the stranded starfish would die if left in the morning sun. "But there must be thousands of beaches and millions of starfish!" exclaimed the young man, "How can you make a difference?" The old man looked at the small starfish, threw it to the safety of the sea, and said, "It makes a difference to this one!"

—AUTHOR UNKNOWN

"There are two ways of exerting one's strength: one is pushing down, the other is pulling up. This is the essence of grace and compassion."
—BOOKER T. WASHINGTON

PREFACE

The title of this book, *Care Enough to Discipline*, is a little misleading. The word "discipline" is often associated with corporal punishment, negative reinforcement, and public humiliation, such as writing the names of erring children on the blackboard. In fact, this little book is based on a call for the positive values on which our country was founded, namely self-discipline, respect for self and others, courage and compassion.

As you will see when you read *Care Enough to Discipline*, the book is a "quick read" and suitable as a guide for busy teachers, parents, and others. The book is divided into 13 brief chapters. These offer the insights of an educator with over 30 years of experience in working with educators and families. Each chapter contains one simple concept, and each chapter stands alone. Thus, it is the sort of book one can begin reading at any point and obtain stimulating thoughts about the care and education of children.

Of particular interest are the appendices. The nine appendices offer numerous quotes from famous classic and contemporary humanists, including Aristotle, Martin Luther King, Antoine de Saint-Exupery, James Comer, and Charles Swindoll, among many others. My favorite is the memorable statement "I have a dream" quote from Martin Luther King's speech. This quote seems to fit the tenor of *Care Enough to Discipline*. I believe Dr. Lane Anderson has a dream of creating, maintaining, and enhancing healthy families and decent children for a democratic society.

One caution: Dr. Anderson is a self-proclaimed maverick. He is not afraid to challenge those educators who do not teach in public schools or psychologists who are too permissive in how to raise responsible children. He blames many of our current social problems on immature people who lack personal responsibility and accountability for their choices.

In sum, I think *Care Enough to Discipline* will appeal to educators, parents, and others who believe that teaching values is the best way to repond to foreign dangers. Dr. Anderson writes in a conversational style based on his own rich experiences. I found the book to be interesting and informative.

—WILLIAM WATSON PURKEY
Professor Emeritus of Counselor Education
The University of North Carolina at Greensboro

ACKNOWLEDGMENTS AND APPRECIATION

Special acknowledgement and appreciation are noted here to some of the many nationally known individuals who have, for many years, consistently promoted and inspired the life lessons of *Care Enough to Discipline*: Oprah Winfrey, Dr. Phil McGraw, Bill Cosby, William Glasser, MD, Dr. Martin Luther King, Jr.,* Dr. John Hope Franklin, James B. Duke, Professor Emeritus of History and Professor of Legal History in the Duke Law School,* Reverend T.D. Jakes, Gloria Steinem, Reverend Rick Warren, Dr. Wayne W. Dyer, Maya Angelou, General Colin Powell, and Stephen R. Covey. Also on a national level, the following educators have had a profound influence on me, as well as a positive impact on overall school improvement throughout our nation: Dr. William Watson Purkey, Professor Emeritus of Counselor Education (UNC - Greensboro) and cofounder of the International Alliance for Invitational Education; James P. Comer, MD, Maurice Falk Professor of Child Psychiatry at Yale University and founder of the Comer School Development Program; Dr. Edward Joyner, Professor of Education at Sacred Heart University and past Executive Director of the Comer School Development Program, Harry and Rosemary Wong, co-authors of *The First Days of School,* the best-selling education book ever on how to be an effective teacher; Dr. Terry Roberts, Executive Director of the National Paideia Center; E. Perry Good, author and consultant for Connected Schools; and Dr. Philip F. Vincent, author and nationally known lecturer on character education.

At the state level, within the North Carolina Department of Public Instruction, I owe special thanks to several leaders who have influenced my work as an educator and consultant: Dr. Craig Phillips, past State Superintendent who served effectively for so many years in that office; Dr. Elsie Leak, past Associate State Superintendent; Marvin Pittman, Community Liaison for Student Achievement, NC State Board of Education; Debora Sydnor, Section Chief for the Raising Achievement and Closing Gaps Section; Marguerite Peebles, Section Chief for the School Safety and Climate Section (character education). On a state association level, special appreciation goes to leaders who influenced many of my views expressed in this book: Michelle Palmer Weaver, Kathleen Wilderman, and Kathy Kennedy—who are all key leaders of the NC Association of Elementary Educators, and John Reimer, President of the NC Dropout Prevention Association.

On a more local level, I want to express gratitude and thanks for the lessons I learned from several remarkable principals with regard to their unique style of leadership and effectiveness in working with students, parents, and staffs: Bob Clendenin, Tim Clifford, Martha Hudson, John Freeman, Tom Lewis, and my wife, "Charlie." Collectively, they were the educational practitioners whom I tried to emulate in all three schools of which I was principal.

Lastly, I want to express appreciation for the professional teachers, outstanding students, and involved parents with whom I had the pleasure to work; they were like second families during my 33 years as a teacher, coach, and principal. They taught me the "real world" principles on which this book is based. And finally, *Care Enough to Discipline* is a tribute to all the great teachers and parents throughout this world who continue to lead by their positive example every day, and never give up on our children.

* *deceased*

GRATITUDE

Though so many friends, teachers, colleagues, life experiences, and a strong faith in God* have made me who I am, my foundation in becoming an adult was laid in pre-school and early childhood.

I am blessed to have a sister, two brothers, terrific children, and wonderful extended family members.

I feel eternally blessed to be married to "Charlie," the love of my life, best friend, and confidant.

I am very grateful to Helen and Lane S. Anderson, Jr., who raised all four of us with love, sacrifice, and discipline. We were fortunate to have parents from truly "the greatest generation."

—L.S.A.

*Trust in the Lord with all your heart and lean not on your own understanding, in all ways acknowledge Him and He will direct thy paths.
—PROVERBS 3:5-6

INTRODUCTION

There are three things that all children need from significant others in their lives at home, school, and community, which are priceless: acceptance, unconditional love, and our time. These needs within children are timeless and relevant to all cultures, ethnic/racial groups, genders, and are not contingent upon socioeconomic circumstances. There are children surviving situations of economic poverty who are advantaged in terms of emotional and psychological support from their families, schools, and communities. There are also some children who come from economic wealth who are disadvantaged because they are living without these support groups so vital for developing positive character and maturity. Many grow up to be successful moneymakers, but not necessarily successful people. Net worth is not self worth despite the images portrayed in the media and accepted societal beliefs about success. Class is not a function of one's economic circumstances or accumulated wealth, but is determined by one's behavior and compassion towards others.

Noble blood is an accident of fortune; noble actions are the chief mark of greatness.
—CARLO GOLDONI (1707-1793)

These noble actions are a result of good character of which discipline is a critical part; doing the right thing at the right time for the right reason. Discipline is about respecting self and others as well as self-control without being indifferent or stoic. It is about growing children into caring adults who exercise good judgment in life.

How we can all contribute to the competence, well-being, and positive growth of our children is the primary focus of this book. It is simply a *guide* on how critical discipline can be in the process of children being taught by the most important teachers in their early life: parents and educators. While many see the discipline process as a result of children avoiding negative consequences in the form of punishment, this book will emphasize discipline more as a function of children *aspiring toward* positive consequences in developing their patterns of behavior.

Lastly, it will be obvious to the reader that this book is *not* a research-based diatribe on the analysis of paradigms, constructs, rubrics, matrixes, charts, and statistical graphs. It is not for the erudite scholars or consultants who have not taught in K-12 public schools, or the "techies" who endlessly analyze data and see numbers rather than children, or anyone with a systems-analyst approach operating from an empirical frame of mind. Rather, it is written as a result of years of input from children, public school teaching staffs, and parents representing the full range of diversity in America. This input is coupled with extensive observations from my experiences of over 33 years working in K-12 schools and constitutes the real world basis upon which the following pages are written. Hopefully, this work will appeal to the common sense of each reader who works with children from the *heart*, which is always a parent's or teacher's greatest guide in raising children for the 21st century anywhere in this wonderful world.

Editorial Warning: All the writing and mistakes in this guide are entirely mine. I can't even blame the staff at Ivy House or the typist/transcriptionist who did their best to advise me on technical errors, some of which I heeded. I cannot thank them enough for their professional skills and patience. Any academician or scholar, publisher, or professional editor would have a field day noting omissions and errors, which would never be made in a more polished work. However, this guide is not intended for erudite analysis by any professional journal in any field or any university publication. Rather, it is intended to be a quick read (less than an hour) by busy educators, parents, and anyone else who truly cares about children. So, *critics*, proceed at your own risk lest you complete the reading of this guide shaking your head in disbelief at its lack of precision, technical correctness, or any other facet which deviates from current thinking or convention.

Note: Chapters will be as succinct as possible because parents and teachers engaged in raising children do not have time to read voluminous publications by self-described *experts*. Remember, "x" is an unknown quantity and a "spurt" is a drip under pressure. Also, many views expressed in this book will be direct, not politically correct. None of the many generalizations or assertions should be construed as absolute truths since there are always exceptions due to the unique diversity among and between all schools and families.

We don't know one millionth of one percent about anything.
—THOMAS ALVA EDISON (1847-1931)

Note: There is extensive use of italics throughout the context of each chapter. This over use of emphasis is meant to give the reader a guide to re-read these words or sentences for maximum retention, understanding, and hopefully, implementation. Also, each chapter text is written in a "conversational" style and does not adhere to strict rules of grammar and syntax.

SUCCESS

Success is in the way you walk
The paths of life each day.
It's in the little things you do
And in the things you say.
Success is not in getting rich
Or rising high to fame.
It's not alone in winning goals
Which all men hope to claim.

Success is being big of heart
And clean and broad of mind.
It's being faithful to your friends
And the stranger kind.

It's in the children that you love
And all they learn from you.
Success depends on character
And everything you do.

—AUTHOR UNKNOWN

Some Philosophical Insights for This Guide

Before I got married I had six theories about bringing up children; now I have six children, and no theories.
—Lord Rochester (1647-1680)

I have a dream my four little children will one day live in a nation where they will not be judged by the color of their skin but by the content of their character.
—Dr. Martin Luther King, Jr.,
"I Have a Dream" speech, 1963

There is no learning without obedience, and there is no obedience without discipline. This relationship in both families and schools must always be based on mutual respect and trust.
—Dr. Lane Anderson

It is not what you do for children but what you have taught them to do for themselves that will make them successful human beings.
—Ann Landers

Suffer the little children to come unto me, and forbid them not: for such is the Kingdom of God
—Mark 10:14

The solution of adult problems tomorrow depends in large measure upon the way our children grow up today. There is no greater insight into the future than recognizing that when we save our children— we save ourselves.
—MARGARET MEAD

What lies behind us and what lies before us are small matters compared to what lies within us.
—RALPH WALDO EMERSON

The great Oxford historian Arnold Toynbee showed in his monumental A Study of History, *that great civilizations are never defeated from the outside. Rather, they decline from the inside . . . It is children who never see peace at home who grow up and fill the world with endless violence and war. You cannot have a peaceful world without having peaceful families.*
—RABBI SHMULEY BOTEACH

It is only with the heart that one can see rightly: what is essential is invisible to the eye.
—ANTOINE DE SAINT-EXUPERY

To be what we are and to become what we are capable of becoming is the only end of life.
—ROBERT LOUIS STEVENSON

Your calling isn't something that somebody can tell you about. It is the thing that gives you juice. The thing that you are supposed to do. And nobody can tell you what that is.
—OPRAH WINFREY, Howard University, 2007

CHAPTER 1
GOOD SCHOOLS, GOOD FAMILIES

A good school is like a good family. The foundation is absolute mutual trust all the time. If this is established, then open and timely communication will follow along with mutual respect for self and others, and a unified commitment toward the common good of others through selfless teamwork. This kind of atmosphere can be established in any home if parents (biological, adoptive, or relatives) care enough to discipline with unconditional love, firmness, respect, and the fairness of consistency. In any good school, teachers become surrogate parents and perceive all students as their own biological children, not someone else's whom they can forget at the end of each instructional day. Based on this premise, each class receives collective instruction, but each student is taught individually based on his/her unique ability and learning style. *Every child is gifted* and talented; disadvantaged and at risk in varying degrees. The mission of parents and educators is to enhance the former and diminish the latter.* Children develop good character when they continuously experience adult role models of compassion, courage, self-discipline, respect, and unconditional love. When good families and good schools work together, children naturally become successful, confident, and caring adults of tomorrow.

*The term "gifted" is used here in the understanding that all children have gifts, which cannot always be quantified by academically based standardized tests. Also, the term "disadvantaged" should not be construed as physical poverty due to poor living conditions, lack of money, tangible possessions, or social status in any class-oriented society. Rather, it means *spiritual* poverty due to the absence of a consistently loving and caring home environment where there is adult leadership and structure based on mutual respect and trust. There are many families of material wealth who are spiritually impoverished.

The most important thing we can teach children is courage: first and foremost, courage to believe in themselves: courage to stand up for and persist in the achievement of worthy ideals no matter what the odds. If we succeed in teaching, mentoring, and sustaining this one facet of character, children's academic competence, compassion, confidence, and commitment will naturally follow.

—Dr. Lane Anderson

CHAPTER 2
THE DIFFERENCE BETWEEN PUNISHMENT
AND DISCIPLINE

There is no learning without obedience, and there is no obedience without discipline. This is a maxim that applies to raising children in families and teaching children in schools. This relationship is always based on mutual trust and respect. Discipline is not the same as punishment. Punishment is normally perceived as a negative consequence for inappropriate behavior and usually associated with physical or emotional pain. It is *externally* applied by accepted or forced authority and has the advantage of being effective with immediate results. Punishment can vary from a spanking by parents in the home or corporal punishment at school to local, federal, or state imprisonment for crimes against society. Often, punitive motivation for correct human behavior is based on avoidance of painful or costly consequences implemented by enforcement, monitoring, or supervision.

In contrast, discipline is positive behavior generated from *within* and takes a long time to develop. It is the key component of character development, which is doing the right thing at the right time for the right reasons *even when no one is looking.* It is exercising good judgment regardless of varying situations, peer pressure, or desire for personal gain. To develop positive character and discipline, children need to continuously be exposed to positive adult role models at home, at school, in churches, synagogues, or mosques, and generally in their community and neighborhood. Since parents are any child's first and greatest teachers, discipline and character based on a desire for doing good always begins in the home and should be reinforced at schools where *all educators* should be positive role models. If this mutual collaboration and support between families and schools is not consistent and continuous with regard to universally accepted core values, then the predictable, structured environment all children need begins to deteriorate, opening the door for control through punishment rather than the development of self-control through discipline.

. . . Discipline is the process by which a child is taught to think properly . . . a child is properly disciplined (or more accurately discipled) by being taught right from wrong and the preferably classical reasons why right is right and wrong is wrong. Discipline, then, is about values.

—JOHN ROSEMOND
Practicing Family Psychologist
Excerpt from his column in the Burlington (NC)
Times-News, May 8, 2009
www.rosemond.com

CHAPTER 3
PARENTING

The most difficult job on earth is being a good parent because there is no universally accepted "how to" manual. There is no warranty whereby you can send children back to the manufacturer for mental or behavioral deficiencies, and the job is 24/7! Children can *enrich* parents' lives beyond measure, but they cannot bring happiness. If this were true, then the parents with the most children would be the happiest people. Children cost a lot of money, add stress to a couples' relationship, and are often inconvenient (babysitters, car pools, planned activities, illnesses, doctor/dentist appointments, etc).

The same can be said of marriage, the most intimate and difficult of human relationships. It is a mistake to marry someone because you want him/her to make you happy. This kind of expectation will eventually lead to disappointment, irritability, resentment, and possible separation/divorce. Another person in a committed relationship can *enrich* your life through shared core values, satisfying mutual emotional/psychological needs, compatibility in having fun together, and being on the same journey toward mutually held dreams. However, each person is always accountable and responsible for his/her own happiness in life. In essence, children are incidental to a marriage, not the reason for it. Of course, it's always best *to be married and stay married* if a couple is going to raise children at least through age 18 (exceptions would be due to ongoing physical, emotional, or psychological abuse). All children deserve two loving parents who care enough to discipline, love them unconditionally, give them time, and accept them for who they are.

Loving children unconditionally does not mean *liking* them all the time. Remember, *discipline is an act of love in caring enough to correct children's natural inclination to make mistakes* and often trying to get away with doing things they shouldn't. This often includes lying, cheating, deceiving, stealing, hitting, disruption, disobedience, disrespect, and a negative attitude. The best guide to being an effective parent is to follow one's heart when correcting a child's behavior, which should never be done in anger and loss of self-control. This almost seems impossible at times because we are all human and sometimes react before we think. But self-control is the hallmark of maturity and if parents act immaturely, there's no leadership in the family and chaotic dysfunction can result.

Being a good parent is the ultimate act of leadership because it involves unconditional love, sacrifice, and suffering for children God and couples bring into this world. But being a couple and biologically bringing a child into the world does not mean being parents (except legally). *A parent is anyone who raises a child on a daily basis.* In addition to being a 24/7 job, *the leadership required in being a good parent is that you always have to be the example of what you want your children to become.*

If parents yell or scream, get drunk or do illegal drugs, physically beat one another, use profanity as a major form of vocabulary, intentionally abuse each other emotionally, dominate/control, or generally act disrespectfully toward their children and each other, that's what their children will observe, live, and sometimes become.* They will develop an insecurity characterized by fear, anger, mistrust, and low self-esteem. What you *tell* children is not nearly as important as the way you *act* around them. Parents need to "walk the talk" or they will lose the respect and obedience of their children because there is a loss of leadership and credibility. Having positional authority does not mean one can lead, especially if that authority is abused. The ultimate test of leadership is to lead by example. Imitation is the greatest form of flattery. *Be* what you want your children to become.

*Note: Occasionally, some children who live in households and/or communities of negative adult role models can, through strong faith and heroic determination, decide to be the opposite of what they experienced early in life. No one knows why two or more children from the same parents, who grew up in the same household/community and attended the same schools, all turn out differently later in life. This is the essence of the ongoing nature vs. nurture debate with regard to influences and other variables in life, which create positive or negative human beings. Most people are composites of both and differ only in degree.

America's Promise For Our Children

In a joint NAESP and National After School Association conference session, General Colin Powell talked about how crucial caring adults are in the development and success of every child: "The success of children starts at home . . . we need to be the simple connection for children . . . every child deserves to be mentored, to be loved, and to be celebrated . . . be the role models of hope children need . . .be 'America's promise' for our children."

From the *Communicator*, monthly newsletter of the National Association of Elementary School Principals (NAESP) May/June, 2009, Volume 32, No. 9

Chapter 4
The Difference Between Teachers and Instructors

As stated earlier, parents are children's first and greatest teachers because students spend less than 14 percent of their waking time in schools every year for formal instruction. This does not count extracurricular activities such as sports, clubs, tutorials, summer school, etc. This is the reason why people who become educators need to realize how critical their impact can be on any child with so little time to truly make a difference.[1]

This is why it is so crucial to have *teachers* in K-12 education, not just *instructors* who are certified in subject area knowledge.* Good instructors are often good presenters and dispensers of knowledge. Their lesson plans are aligned with state-mandated curriculum objectives by subject and/or grade level, often called standard courses of study. Instructors are effective at *covering the material* and training students in specific areas of knowledge, which will be asked on standardized tests. They are often referred to as *cookbook teachers* because they follow lesson plans like a recipe, rarely deviating off track into teachable moments of inquiry from students. Emphasis is on *right* answers.

The instructor/training approach is effective, especially in the early K-5 grades where so many fundamentals in math

[1] National Association of Elementary School Principals, *Principal Magazine,* Sept/Oct 2004, page 6.

and reading must be mastered before higher order learning can occur. But *teachers* transcend mere training of fundamentals and constantly challenge students with "what if" questions, thereby motivating students to learn through independent self-discovery. They know that the goal of training is to teach something specific while education is the *application* of training to solve unique problems long into the future. Teachers instruct classes of students collectively, but then circulate among students and *differentiate* instruction by leaning over each student for one-on-one assistance depending upon varied learning styles and baselines of knowledge. This is when motivation occurs, which is the critical art/skill of great teachers. They know how to go inside each child's potential and bring out the best, thereby instilling confidence, perseverance, and ultimately self-esteem and success. All great teachers are also good instructors, but not all good instructors are necessarily effective teachers.

Instructors can be trained in methods courses in university schools of education, but great teachers are *born* to do what they do best as virtually an art form, which can't be taught from any textbook of pedagogy. The great ones are "called" into the profession because of their natural love for children of any age, which includes caring enough to discipline. They instinctively know that character development is just as important as academic competency and they teach both simultaneously through their constant, personal example of leadership. In essence, *the teacher is the curriculum in any classroom!*

Finally, great teachers have several universal characteristics (four "Cs"), which are often not seen within the sample evidences and functional categories of instructor performance evaluation instruments used by administrators during classroom observations. First is *competence*, not only in subject areas as certified by university training, but in the ability to *naturally* relate to students so that classroom management is not a problem. Second is *confidence*, which is a demeanor and personal bearing by which teachers communicate that they are in charge, know what they are doing, and have high expectations for *every* student with regard to both behavior and academic achievement. Third is *compassion*, which is an authentic empathy (not sympathy) for the feelings of each student. They understand each student without a "bleeding heart" syndrome, which often enables some students to remain victims of their circumstances or disabilities. Again, teachers care enough to discipline and accept no excuses for less than the best from every child. The fourth "C" of great teachers is absolute *commitment* to persevere through patience and the belief that every child can succeed. They never become jaded, cynical, or *burned out** (unless there is a lack of administrative leadership or support) and never allow a student to give up on himself/herself. They are continuously *energized* by every student who improves every day in their classrooms.

Lastly, if you wrap the four "Cs" of great teachers with *enthusiasm* and a *sense of humor*, you have a leader who will be effective with children. They take their job seriously, but not themselves. Teachers remain cool under pressure because they do not internalize (take personally) the strange or immature things students do, especially good-natured class clowns. They laugh *with* their students but never *at* them, taking care never to embarrass or humiliate. The joy they exude while teaching becomes contagious enthusiasm and motivates children to learn while also having fun! All successful parents are like effective teachers. We need more great parents and teachers if America is to remain strong and free enough to sustain the ideals of democracy and world peace.

*Mediocre instructors never burn out because they are working for a paycheck, benefits, and retirement. Sometimes the great teachers can burn out because they are idealists and care about every student. When they are not supported by administration or parents, they can develop chronic fatigue and even depression.

Let us not confuse teaching with learning, grade advancement with education, a diploma with competence, or fluency with the ability to say something new.
—John Oligher, 1970

Our greatest contribution is to be sure there is a teacher in every classroom who cares that every student, every day, learns and grows and feels like a real human being.
—The Gallup Organization
Education Mission Statement, 1979

In a completely rational society, the best of us would aspire to be teachers and the rest of us would have to settle for something less, because passing civilization along from one generation to the next ought to be the highest honor and the highest responsibility anyone could have.
—Lee Iacocca, Former Chrysler Chairman

CHAPTER 5
STRUCTURES, EXPECTATIONS, FAIRNESS

As mentioned in the introduction, all children need our acceptance, unconditional love, and time. Acceptance is honoring and supporting the unique characteristics and talents that naturally develop within each child in a *positive* direction. It does not mean acceptance of inappropriate behaviors. In this reagard, unconditional love does not mean parents or educators *like* everything children say or do. Finally, giving our time to raise children at home or school does not mean that all our free time necessarily revolves around their natural self-centeredness. There must always be a reasonable balance of time and attention so that children do not become spoiled or develop an attitude of entitlement or the arrogance of always expecting to get their way.

This balance begins with *structure*, both at home and at school. Structures are the parameters and boundaries established by parents in the home and educators in schools. Since good schools are like good families, their respective structures ensure cooperation and consideration in living and working with others by adhering to schedules as well as rules of "dos and don'ts" of behaviors. Closely aligned with structures are expectations of parents and educators for everyone living and working within these authoritative* environments. The reasonableness of both structures and expectations are based on timeless, universally accepted values as well as age-appropriateness and accountability. For example, a three year old at home can pick up his/her things and store them in designated areas, but would have difficulty vacuuming or doing his/her own laundry. However, nine to 18-year-olds can keep their rooms clean, make their beds, clean bathrooms, help with dinner, do dishes, do their laundry, and assist with outside chores as long as they live in their parents' homes.

At schools, each grade level and each classroom must have relevant structures, expectations, and schedules with regard to acceptable behavior, obedience to authority, assigned academic work, cooperation, consideration for others, attendance, required timelines for completing assignments, as well as schedules which dictate movement anywhere in the school. Without unified adherence to reasonable structures and expectations, both homes and schools can quickly become dysfunctional and chaotic. *When anything goes, everything goes.*

Fairness is the key to blending structure with expectations because it involves applied *consequences* when children go outside the boundaries of structure or fall short of expectations. Without consequences there is no modification of negative behavior toward acceptable behavior and character development. *Consistency* is the hallmark of this process and the essence of fairness. If one child is corrected with a resulting consequence and another is not, then inconsistency erodes the credibility of whoever is leading (parents or educators). Children possess an innate sense of fairness and it is one of the primary yardsticks by which they measure adults and build trust. If that trust is betrayed over and over again, then a structure of inconsistency and unpredictability engenders a feeling of insecurity within children. Insecurity is what fosters a lack of maturity which manifests itself by a lack of self-control, impulsive reaction, low self-esteem, and an inability to defer gratification. There should always be a wide range of consequences for inappropriate behaviors so that the adult on the scene (closest to the problem) can administer the most appropriate consequence(s) depending on the frequency and severity of incidents. It is essential that knowledge of consequences for disobedience, disrespect, and disruption be understood well in advance of having to use them. This develops accountability in children to take responsibility for their actions and is also a part of fairness and discipline.

Note: Sometimes, positive reinforcement (recognition, rewards, privileges, etc.) can more effectively encourage appropriate behavior than negative consequences, especially as children become more mature. The ideal goal is consistently "positive" behavior based on character; doing the right thing or acting the right way simply because it is right, not to avoid negative consequences or receive rewards.

*Authoritative is used here to indicate positional authority based on caring, compassion, and empathy. This is opposed to the word *authoritarian*, which is positional authority based on power, force, and enforcement of unreasonable rules and policies, usually for purposes of absolute control.

Building a Better Family

Seven Deadly Habits of Family Relating	Seven Habits for Happy Family Relating
I recognize that when I try to exert external control over you, it only serves to decrease the quality of the relationship between us. Therefore, I commit to no longer do the following:	Instead, I recognize that I can only control my own behavior. Therefore, I commit to doing those behaviors that build stronger relationships between you and me as follows:
Criticize you	Support you
Blame you	Encourage you
Complain to you	Listen to you
Nag you	Accept you
Threaten you	Trust you
Punish you	Respect you
Reward to control you	Settle differences with you

—William Glasser, MD, 2003

CHAPTER 6
SETTING UP STRUCTURE AND ESTABLISHING EXPECTATIONS FOR FAIRNESS AND CHILDREN'S SUCCESS THROUGH CONSISTENT DISCIPLINE

There are infinite combinations of effective structures, expectations, and consequences in both schools and families because one size does not fit all. Parents and educators must follow their hearts, their core values, experience, and sense of fairness in the process of establishing structures that promote adherence to reasonable expectations for children's behaviors. This could range from charts for chores and a discipline matrix at home to a formalized discipline code signed by parents, children, and staff in schools. The key is a common understanding (not necessarily agreement) of what is expected within the boundaries of either environment.

Consistency in administering consequences for inappropriate behaviors will determine the degree of predictability to sustain continuous positive behaviors over time. Each home and school must ensure that there is no deviation from age-appropriate expectations within established boundaries of structure. All adults (one or more parents or an entire school staff) must be absolutely *unified* in this regard or children will see inconsistency in the application of corrections and consequences, which will erode trust, credibility, and inner personal security. Parenting and teaching are the most difficult, ultimate acts of leadership because of multiple split second decisions and because adults in these positions must continuously exemplify, through their actions and words, the kind of persons they want their children to become.

The great Oxford historian, Arnold Toynbee, showed in his monumental A Study of History *that great civilizations are never defeated from the outside. Rather, they decline from the inside . . . It is children who never see peace at home who grow up and fill the world with endless violence and war. You cannot have a peaceful world without having peaceful families.*
—RABBI SHMULEY BOTEACH

Chapter 7
Character

If parents and teachers continuously love children enough to discipline them in the manner stated in the previous chapters, our society would continuously improve because we would develop young people who understand and live courage, compassion, perseverance, the ethic of hard work and doing one's best, as well as consideration and respect for self and others at all times. All the great religions of the world teach these central core values through scriptures of respect, brotherhood, tolerance, and the golden rule. They only differ in religious procedures, the depiction of God, and the question of what constitutes life after death. In essence, if *everyone* would actually *practice* the tenets of the world's great religions and denominations, we would have a world united in both character and peaceful, prosperous coexistence. Though there are many books on the subject of character development, I offer a succinct encapsulation of yet another definition of my own:

> *Character is doing the right thing at the right time for the right reasons. Leadership is character in action in service to others. We manage things and lead people.*
>
> *Character cannot be taught from a book but only by the personal example of significant others (e.g. positive role models). The antithesis of character results when negative role models are emulated because striving in a positive di-*

rection is perceived to be too difficult, too dull, or too slow in fulfilling one's needs or life ambitions.

There is an inverse correlation between character and self-centeredness. Compassion, empathy, and altruism are the emotional qualities of character and provide purpose to outward actions.

To a person with character, obstacles and difficulties in life are perceived as challenges that can be overcome with confidence, optimism, and persistence. Overcoming adversity is the chief means through which character is developed. The result is always increased self-esteem, which is essential if one is to have the character to love and give to others.

Courage and judgment are also essential components of character. To stand up for one's ideals, no matter how difficult the circumstances, requires fortitude based on a core set of positive values. The judgment to assess and act in difficult and "gray" areas in life situations requires a decisiveness which can only come from character continuously strengthened by time and experience.

If there could be universal and general agreement on the basic intention and concept of the foregoing encapsulation, we would have homes and schools of caring, mature adults raising caring, mature children with courage, compassion, and good judgment. Children who grow into adults with character are resilient, confident, competent, cooperative, self-reliant, considerate, and competitive through teamwork. These are essential characteristics for success in both life and work. Maintaining a technological edge in a global economy is important, but the *people who manage the technology* and lead our families, businesses, and government institutions are critical in making it all work for the common good of everyone.

Good judgment comes from experience and experience comes from poor judgment.
—ANONYMOUS

Human potential, though not always apparent, is there waiting to be discovered and invited forth.
—DR. WILLIAM PURKEY

When things get tough always remember . . . faith doesn't get you around trouble, it gets you through it! When you relinquish the desire to control your future, you obtain happiness.
—ANONYMOUS

DR. LANE S. ANDERSON

Obama to Fathers: Be Involved

In a personal Father's Day weekend message on June 19, President Obama encouraged all fathers to be involved in their children's lives. Citing the emotional fallout when his own dad, Barack Obama, Sr., left the home when Barack Obama, Jr. was only two, President Obama commented that his dad's absence left a "hole in his heart." He credits the heroic role models of other family members for his success: "I had a heroic mom and wonderful grandparents who helped raise me and my sister, and it's because of them that I am able to stand here today . . . but despite all of their extraordinary love and attention, that doesn't mean that I didn't feel my father's absence. That's something that leaves a hole in a child's heart that a government can't fill."

From an Associated Press article
syndicated in the *Burlington Times-News* (NC),
June 21, 2009.

CHAPTER 8
FIVE MAJOR INFLUENCES ON CHILDREN'S DEVELOPMENT

Parents and immediate family members are the first and most influential teachers in any child's development. Critical brain formation, emulation of positive/negative behaviors, development of core values, social interaction skills, respect for self and others, and basic development of discipline, maturity (self-control), as well as readiness for structured learning environments (pre-school, kindergarten), are all dependent upon family environments. The infinite combination of variables unique to each family environment is what makes for such great diversity of maturity and learning readiness in the early grades (pre-K to third) of formal schooling. Add to this mix the differences in cultural, racial, and ethnic influences and one can see the complexity, which has impact on both our schools and communities. It is all the more reason to be *unified* on *universally* accepted values and character development noted in earlier chapters among and between parents and educators. When there is incongruence or inconsistency in this regard due to lack of communication and respect, then misunderstandings are often manifested by conflict, racism, and deterioration of trust.

Secondly, the surrounding community in which a child grows up has tremendous impact on his/her development. This includes neighborhoods, churches, safety of play areas, and the compassion of city/county governments, especially school boards, city councils, and county commissioners. Equity in access to opportunities for positive growth throughout a child's community has a definite impact on whether or not a child develops *hope* in bettering himself/herself through schools and organizations beyond his/her home environment.

Thirdly, and closely allied to surrounding community influences, are friends, groups, gangs, athletic teams, and after-school activities (including summer vacation time). This peer influence is particularly crucial in grades five through eight, as children naturally become less compliant toward parents and established authority. It is generally the time when children want to create their own unique identities, as well as become part of a like-minded group of friends, which could represent a positive or negative set of values. Ironically, the middle grades are when parents often begin to become less involved when it is really the time to become more involved!

The best guidance is to *supervise, supervise, supervise!* Of course, children at these ages will resent being treated, well, like children in early elementary school. "Helicopter" parents are overly involved because they hover over and micromanage everything their children do, grooming them for pre-conceived goals (sometimes kids become alter egos for their parents or family traditions of expectation). Other parents begin to back off to the point of becoming overly permissive, either due to a lack of energy (will fatigue) or even a subliminal fear of being too hard on their children. An ideal position is somewhere near the middle in most situations. This means the authoritative position of the parent/teacher is the last word, but there can be a latitude of choices a child can make within the boundaries of the family or school structure. This compromise provides opportunities for any child to develop *autonomy* through developing good judgment within a range of acceptable parameters. The key is knowing when to be the "gorilla" in your child's perception without feeling guilty and when to allow your child to make good choices or mistakes that are not dangerous or life threatening. There is no manual on the art of parenting during these "difficult years," but a parent must lead from a strong position of both positive values and character.

The fourth greatest influence in raising children is the quality of the schools, which children attend from pre-K to graduating seniors in high school. This quality is determined by the dedication of the overall administration (principals, assistant principals, grade level or department heads, and secretarial staff) and whether or not the adults teaching your children are instructors or genuine teachers (see chapter four). If these factors are positive in any school, regardless of location, racial/ethnic diversity, or economic levels, then the school will become like a *second family* where there is absolute trust, open and timely communication, respect for self and others, and unified commitment to the positive development of each and every unique child.

All great schools are like great families where every adult is a role model and a *consistent* example for children to emulate regardless of their respective, multiculturally diverse backgrounds. This *consistency of caring*, dedication, adherence to school-wide policies and procedures, professional competence, and positive character are the primary responsibilities of the administrative leadership. This means that all the universally accepted principles of character are also part of the overall curriculum objectives taught for academic competence.

By law, academic competence in public schools is measured through quarterly benchmark testing, weekly tests, final exams, adequate yearly progress (AYP), and year-end standardized testing required by federal and state laws. However, there is no quantitative measure of good character within each student, only observed behaviors, referrals to in-school suspension centers, or administrative suspension/expulsion for violations of school district codes of conduct. *The great irony is that what cannot be measured* (discipline/character) *drives what does get measured* (tests/exams). *Great teachers are the instructional leaders in every school and are the real curriculum in every classroom.* The curriculum objectives written in standard courses of study and subject area department manuals/pacing guides are only the *medium* through which teachers teach children. When asked what they do, all the great teachers say they teach children first, followed by their respective grade levels and subject area specialty. They are individuals of great professional competence and great character who understand the duality of their skills and personal leadership in developing the *whole* student: "Educating the mind without educating the heart is no education at all." (Aristotle). Most people who recall the two or three best teachers in their schooling would probably fail a final exam given by these teachers if they took these tests today, but they will never forget the *personal example* of these teachers' caring, discipline style, and consistent expectations for excellence from every student.

Though good schools and great teachers contribute to the positive development of every child, the *window of time* that schools have to impact children is surprisingly very narrow. If one figures an average six-hour instructional day for a 180-day school year and factors out summer school and after-school activities (athletics, clubs, tutorial), children spend an average of *less than 14 percent of their waking hours in schools!**

This means that the other aforementioned influences of immediate family, community/neighborhood, and each student's peer groups have a substantially more impact on a child's holistic growth than K-12 schools. However, when things go badly and trust is eroded between schools and families, parents often blame the schools, school staffs blame parents, and everybody blames TV, video games, the Internet, and the media. But fixing the blame instead of fixing the problem doesn't solve anything and only widens achievement gaps and erodes communication and trust.

This leads to the *fifth* and *final determination of success in both families and schools*, which is the child himself/herself! Even if the other four major influences are positive environments, *each child is ultimately accountable and responsible for his/her own success and happiness* not only during school years but also throughout life itself! This premise is a major paradigm shift for many parents and possibly American culture, which often believes that the right amount of money, number of possessions (for show or convenience), or the right pill will bring contentment, character, and happiness. If this were true, *all* the top stars in professional sports and the entertainment industry, as well as the CEOs of the Fortune 500 companies, would be the happiest people on earth. Conversely, there are many examples of children of poverty (regardless of race, gender, or ethnicity) who grew up in what may be considered dysfunctional families, attended low performing schools, and were considered "disadvantaged" children, who became people of great character, and can be considered successful parents with middle to wealthy incomes. This is an illustration of why *equal opportunity in America does not mean equal outcome*. Taking advantage of increasing opportunities now guaranteed by civil rights legislation since the mid-1960s means having a strong work ethic, perseverance, courage, positive character and self-esteem, a willingness to try, reasonable conformity to institutional policies, procedures, and laws while also maintaining individuality and pride in one's ethnic heritage.

Of the five major influences just described in creating successful children, a child's *immediate family* remains the greatest predictor of life success. There are many economically advantaged children who attend the finest schools who sometimes become successful moneymakers, but not successful people. Conversely, there are children who are economically impoverished, but who come from families of spiritual wealth, unconditional love and caring discipline who are successful in school and who become successful people both financially and as parents. Maybe the wealthiest people are not the ones who have the most, but the ones who need the least.

*Based on a six-hour instructional day and assuming eight hours of sleep per night and a 180-day school year, a student spends only about *13.36* percent of his or her waking hours in *school* by age 18. NAESP *Principal Magazine,* Sept./Oct. 2004, p. 6.

Maybe the Problem Starts at Home

If the children are out of control, it is simply because parents have given over control. God can and will help you train your children. Just ask him. Also, read his manual on child training. It's called Proverbs.

—PASTOR J. MARK FOX,
Antioch Community Church, Elon, (NC)
From a weekly column in the Burlington (NC)
Times-News, December 1, 2007

CHAPTER 9
"NO CHILD LEFT BEHIND" AND
ASSESSING THE WHOLE VILLAGE

Since about 86 percent of major influences on children's development is *outside* schools, it is unfair to hold educators *totally* accountable for the academic success of all children. This is why the federally mandated "No Child Left Behind" (NCLB) legislation, though well intentioned, is unreasonable and unfair. Many students cannot meet the higher testing standards for promotion and we are "burning out" many of our best teachers, especially the ones wanting to work with our most "at risk" learners. The reason is that NCLB requires 100 percent adequate yearly progress (AYP) for *every* student sub-group in a school (some high risk schools have 20 to 25 sub-groups due to extreme diversity of need.) These educators are doing their best, are often up against impossible odds, but are made to feel that somehow they are failing children who don't pass largely due to the negative influences on children during the eighty-six percent of time they are out of school! If it "takes a whole village" to raise a child, then maybe we ought to evaluate the rest of the village's other four major influences (see chapter eight) with an assessment score on: (a) whether or not parents are sending us *teachable children* as well as their involvement and support of the schools, (b) whether or not county commissioners and legislators are adequately funding the need for more classroom space, materials, adequate salaries/supplements for teachers, and monies to ensure lower student/teacher ratios (the best key to improving academic achievement), (c) whether or not the surrounding neighborhoods/communities where children live are nurturing or a negative influence (especially peer groups) and finally, (d) whether or not the student, himself or herself, is behaving with respect for self and others, showing up for school and class on time, is obeying teachers, administrators, as well as school-wide expectations (policies, programs, procedures), paying attention in class, turning in homework, and doing their best to prepare for testing and exams.

Remember, the "it takes a whole village to raise a child" works fine in third world, underdeveloped countries where many people really *do* live in villages. However, this phrase is not an appropriate metaphor for highly industrialized, competitive nations, which are entrepreneurial, covet wealth and possessions, and value individualized ownership of property in urban, suburban, and rural settings.

CHAPTER 10
CONSEQUENCES

At the beginning of this guide, there was a stated premise that there is no learning without obedience and no obedience without discipline. Generally, there are three negative behaviors that children can exhibit both at home and school (the three Ds): *disobedience, disrespect, and disruption.* Sometimes one violation is a combination of all three (for example: assault is disobedience of the law/school rules, disrespects the rights of another, and can be disruptive in a home, school, and someone's life. Only one rule is essential in a family home or in any K-12 school: *we respect ourselves and others at all times.* If everyone (parents, children, school staff) and society acted on this one principle all the time, we would have no school suspensions and few social problems. It is analogous to the "golden rule," which is learned in virtually every major religion at an early age.

However, *knowing* the expectations of appropriate behavior and *living* the principles of good character (see chapter seven) is difficult for even the most mature individual all the time. Though there should be a direct correlation between increasing age and improving character and behavior, observation by parents and educators shows that there is often an *inverse* correlation. For example, children are fairly compliant (psychological disorders excepted) until about nine years old and around fourth grade. Just videotape class changes in an elementary school (as opposed to a middle/high school) for a few days and then analyze the differences in behaviors. In many homes, parents wonder "what happened to our child?!" about the ages of nine or ten. If maturity is compliance with reasonable laws and universal principles of conduct (civility, manners, compassion for others, cooperation, etc.) and self-control through positive self-esteem, then children *and* adults should become more mature as they get older. Most readers, through their own observations, know that quite the opposite often occurs.

The only way to modify negative behaviors toward the consistency of positive behaviors (character) is through *both* negative consequences and positive reinforcement by those in positional authority (parents, school staffs, law enforcement, court systems, and elected/appointed legislators). Negative consequences are those that simply punish for the sake of public safety, societal decency, or for maintaining order in our communities, public buildings and institutions. Consequences of positive reinforcement (rewards), though not always an easy process, are intended to improve character by withholding *privileges, which must be earned everyday through positive actions of character.*

For example, most people agree that incarceration in jails or prisons does not always rehabilitate criminals, especially those with life terms and no parole. However, restrictions of freedom of movement in a home or school can be time out, in-school suspension, grounding, no car keys for a while, or being "benched" on an athletic team or cheerleading squad. The underlying premise for either positive or negative consequences is that *every freedom* allowed by law or social boundaries is a privilege (not a right), which *requires an equal amount of responsibility and accountability for one's actions.* Adherence to our Constitution and Bill of Rights requires character and decent behavior or these documents would simply become words amidst a diversity of self-centered interpretation and chaos. This is why we have laws, courts, and a Supreme Court. If a child or an adult develops an attitude of "entitlement" for freedoms without responsibility or unrealistic economic expectations without hard work and perseverance, then we have dysfunctional behaviors in homes, schools, and in society. *When anything goes, everything goes.*

Consequences in homes need to be age-appropriate, immediate, and consistent whether administered by one or both parents. It is imperative that parents back each other 100 percent and only disagree in private later, never in front of children. This is a unified front and promotes inner security within children even if they don't like the consequences. If your heart or faith condones corporal punishment (spanking), make sure it is done *before* a child is five or six, always below the waist with an open hand, and never in anger (loss of self-control, which is the opposite of maturity). The intention of *compassionate* corporal punishment is never to inflict pain or injury but simply to establish who's in charge and temporarily humiliate since small children still have a desire to please their parents and be accepted. This is different from the term "hitting," which can be violent, meant to do bodily harm, and is usually done above the waist and most times aimed at the head or face.

In schools, there should always be a sequential, age-appropriate discipline plan in every classroom with a copy in the principal's/assistant principal's office. These can range from simple reminders and warnings to in-room timeouts, isolation, or loss of privileges related to the classroom. Referral outside the classroom to the principal's office or in-school suspension area should always be a last resort action by a teacher. This can be done in order to preserve a safe, orderly, and respectful learning environment and to protect the rights of all the other students to pursue their opportunity to learn. In-school suspension centers (see next chapter) should always have tutorial and counseling components to complete work missed in class and for attitude adjustments or there will be no change in the referred student's behavior. Out of school suspension, which is always the prerogative of the school administration, is a negative consequence that is only used as a last resort to preserve an orderly and safe learning environment. Sometimes, a set number of referrals to the office or in-school suspension center dictate such action. The key to implementing consequences for negative behaviors, either in schools or in the home, is that *children have knowledge beforehand and that there is consistency* (fairness) and immediacy of administering these known consequences regardless of gender, race, ethnicity, or socioeconomic class. Discriminatory favoritism by either parents or educators erodes credibility in the eyes of children, and is a betrayal of trust, which fosters a sense of alienation and frustration or anger within children.

Remember, the best way to motivate children to choose appropriate behaviors based on the principles of character is to have them *earn* their freedoms and "wants" every day. This is often called *positive reinforcement*, which means getting something they want if preceding behavior warrants it. For example, there can be a movie on the weekend if family or school behavior is consistently good, or if grades are acceptable, a child can participate in after-school activities. Safe driving means use of a car, but this is restricted if there is a moving violation or a betrayal of trust. Most children are more effectively motivated by positive reinforcement because they develop an understanding that positive behaviors earn positive rewards, which creates high self-esteem, responsibility, and good judgment in making right choices in life. Exercising good judgment through character and the maturity of self-control is the primary objective of both parents and educators because the result is an adult who becomes a productive citizen in society and an individual with courage to stand up for worthy ideals, while also having the compassion to help others in need.

It is not what you do for children but what you have taught them to do for themselves [and others] that will make them successful human beings.
—ANN LANDERS

CHAPTER 11
PARENTS & EDUCATORS AS *COACHES* & *REFS*

If character is doing the right thing at the right time for the right reasons (especially if no one is looking) and maturity is about self-control (discipline), then the *hallmark of positive human development is holding one's self responsible and accountable for one's behaviors.* As long as children or adults *blame others* (parents, peers, siblings, educators) or institutions (government, law enforcement, schools, employers, etc.) for their own inappropriate behaviors, they cannot lead themselves, much less others. Immaturity always laments that "it's not my fault," "don't blame me," "they're racist," "they don't like me," or even worse, "they made me do it." Though we can't always control what happens to us in life (unhappy situations, tragedies, unfairness, unreasonable people), we *can* control our reactions to negative situations through being *proactive in positive responses and choices.*

Except in declarations of war or being physically assaulted, using negative, inappropriate actions to fight negative situations only escalates the intensity of the issue at hand. For example, if children want to avoid being corrected by parents or educators, then they need to learn to do what is expected or do what they are told *without warnings or reminders.*

Great parents and educators are like "refs" in sports. If a child steps out of bounds or violates a rule, the "ref" is going to blow the whistle and consistently apply the appropriate consequence. Family policies and procedures at home, as well as discipline policies and procedures at school, are the *play-books* that determine expected behaviors of children. Educators and parents are the *coaches* who judge how well the players (children) are running the plays. Good coaches provide encouragement and guidance because of their maturity, leadership, and expertise, but they also administer team (family/school) sanctions and consequences consistently and fairly as needed because they *care*. Again, discipline is about caring if it is done from the heart in the interest of a child's future success as a human being.

Every child who has ever played on a team will admit that they didn't always *like* their coaches, but respected their authority to correct and make adjustments to make individual players and the team better every game. If coaches and parents don't care enough to discipline, then players (children) don't care enough to obey or improve by working harder. Though consequences, penalties, sanctions, and corrections are often difficult, coaches, "refs," and parents know that they are necessary to succeed in competition and the game of life. If there are no rules or boundaries, there is dysfunction and chaos. Once any child (player) accepts responsibility and accountability for his/her actions, then maturity and good judgment improve. *Sincere ownership* of mistakes or inappropriate behavior means there will be no repetition or excuses in the future. If there is repetition, consequences must be applied to the point where inappropriate behavior ceases to be cost effective. Every person should apologize to anyone whom they have hurt or offended whether their action(s) were intentional or unintentional. The *sincerity* of any apology is reflected in future actions which do not repeat the negative behavior. Otherwise, a verbal apology is meaningless and only meant as an appeasement with no intention of behaving better in the future. If repetition of inappropriate behavior continues, eventually a child has to experience *temporary exclusion* from the family (time out, restrictions of privileges) or schooling process (removal from the classroom), which is the topic of the next chapter.

Note: Three of the greatest coaches who influenced my life on and off the field/court were Stuart Allen (track), George Powell (basketball), and Gus Purcell (football). They were like surrogate dads who demanded the best of us as players and students at Myers Park High School in the early 1960s.* *How* we played each game in competition was jsut as important as winning. It was all about the collective character of integrated teamwork!
Charlotte, North Carolina

CHAPTER 12
EXCLUSION: TIME OUT & THE CARE CENTER

As mentioned earlier, there are no "rights" or freedoms without personal responsibility and accountability for choices and behaviors. Many children and immature adults believe that irresponsible actions constitute personal freedom and are self-centered enough to also believe that there should be no consequences or accountability for their actions. For example, we all have the freedom to drive anywhere in the United States, but we must have a valid driver's license, adhere to directions from road signs, and abstain from driving under the influence of alcohol or drugs. Also, we all have the freedom to "party" in our homes or public establishments, but have the responsibility not to use illegal drugs, not to mix prescription drugs with alcohol, nor to get "drunk" and drive as determined by legal limits in our blood streams. Behavior outside these legal limits and boundaries will often result in negative legal consequences and/or physiological/mental damage to our health and possibly others.

The most frequent excuse of immature people in this regard is *blaming* the influences of substances for their irresponsible behaviors. "I was so drunk or so under the influence of drugs that I didn't know what I was doing." That doesn't even make sense to them when they're sober and trying to be contrite for previous, inappropriate conduct.

Aside from the obvious human behaviors that break the

laws of society in the name of personal "rights" and freedoms, let's focus on typical, negative behaviors of children within schools and families, which are being disobedient, disrespectful, or disruptive (remember the three Ds). When these behaviors occur, there must be immediate and consistent consequences (fairness) by parents and educators. As mentioned earlier, all consequences should match the severity and frequency of the negative behaviors based on the best *judgment* of the adults in charge at home or school (our metaphorical coaches and "refs"). Though a parent or educator's judgment may not always be perfect in certain circumstances or "close plays" of children's behavior, their "call" (judgment) cannot be questioned at the time consequences or directives are given. Otherwise, they end up in endless negotiation and explanation with children, who naturally are trying to evade what they are being told to do. These kinds of discussions can always be held upon later reflection *after* a child completes a given task or an assigned consequence for inappropriate behaviors.

If negative behaviors become repetitious, at some point parents or educators must use *exclusion* from normal family functions or the schooling process. In families, this exclusion is normally the phrase: "Go to your room" or some form of time out. In today's "plugged in" digital world, sending any child to his/her room is like a free ticket to an amusement park or entertainment center complete with TVs, DVDs, iPods, the Internet, and of course cell phones. This only puts a child out of sight, but not truly isolated for needed reflection. An effective time out should not only be solitary confinement, but extremely boring to maximize self-reflection about one's own behavior during a slow passage of time. It's also a message that behavior must become positive before a child earns the right to the freedom of being with the family again or allowed back in a classroom. In a home, it should be a safe area where the child sits in isolation on a wooden stool or chair (no cushions) and told not to move until given permission (take care of bathroom needs beforehand). Parents should check on their child periodically for safety, but if the child is off the stool/chair, then 15 minutes is *added* to the time the parent had in mind initially. The same "penalty box" rule applies if a child makes any noise or is disruptive in any way. A utility room is ideal for time out as the only entertainment is to stare at the washer/dryer combination. Keep in mind that detergents, cleaners, and other chemicals are safely stored and out of reach, again for safety reasons for young children. Usually, an appropriate time out for children under five is about 20 minutes, unless they violate the rules of conduct for time out or if they repeat misbehaviors more than once or twice in the same day. As a child gets older, the maximum time out can be extended. Believe me, there is very little benefit for this kind of cost for any child who *chooses* to disobey, disrespect, or be disruptive in any family environment. This kind of isolated time out can also be an *added* consequence if there is misbehavior outside the home such as in stores, restaurants, daycares, or schools.

Since schools are institutional environments, time out or exclusion has to be a consistent *consequence as a last resort* for disobedience, disrespect, or disruption. In really great schools, all staff members (administrators, teachers, classroom assistants, custodians, cafeteria workers, etc.) are surrogate parents outside the immediate families of their students, but care just as much. Remember, discipline is an act of love and caring, especially in K-12 schools, but it must be consistent to be fair to all students.

Exclusion in any school is based on the democratic philosophy that a good education is everyone's "right" as long as each individual's behavior does not infringe on or detract from everyone else's opportunity for a free and appropriate education or a teacher's right to teach in a positive, safe, and respectful learning environment. As soon as there is repetition of misconduct and the sequence of age-appropriate classroom consequences prove to be ineffective for any child, someone has to leave the room, and it's not going to be the teacher.

Most schools have what is called an in-school suspension program (ISS), a place where usually less than ten percent of students are sent to complete their class work, receive some counseling, and commit to a contract of no further misbehavior. To be effective, ISS programs must have a highly skilled ISS director who is respected (not feared) by students and an administration that backs the judgment of school staff in the referring process. Otherwise, an ISS program can become a "revolving door" joke because this type of consequence does not motivate more positive behavior.

One example of an effective ISS program is a concept called the **Center for Academic and Reflective Education**© (CARE Center), which has the following characteristics:

1) An excellent director who is respected by students, staff, and parents.

2) A serious learning environment where tutoring can occur to complete work not being done in class.

3) A referral to administration for out-of-school suspension if a student continues misbehavior in the CARE Center.

4) Immediate phone contact to a parent or guardian at the time of referral to the CARE Center.

5) A copy of the referral form goes home with the stu-

dent, one is put in the referring teacher's box, and one filed for administration.

6) Copies of referrals are mailed to parents/guardians for instances when phone contact cannot be made.

7) A referral log, alphabetically by teacher, to reflect date/time of referred students, coded offense, and frequency of referral.

8) More than three referrals to the CARE Center in each nine-week quarter results in an automatic one-day suspension out of school on the third referral and for every referral thereafter (stops the revolving door). The slate is clean at the beginning of each quarter.

9) Warning letters are sent to parents/guardians after a second referral due to an automatic out-of-school suspension on the third referral within each quarter.

10) The school's discipline code, operating expectations, and CARE Center referral process must be read and signed by both parents/guardians and students during the first week of school to avoid misunderstanding.*

The concept of the CARE Center in schools really works to guarantee a safe and orderly learning environment for students and staff, as well as assure all parents that repetitive disobedience, disrespect, or disruption will not be tolerated. It is critical that all parents/guardians understand that *they* are responsible and accountable for sending a "teachable child" to school or the child will be home with them until *their home consequences* are effective in creating a more cooperative student. Schools do not physically punish students, "ground" them, or unplug all their digital devices. Only parents can implement these consequences. All schools should use out-of-school suspension as a last resort to guarantee everyone's right and opportunity to learn in a safe, caring, orderly learning environment. Obviously, we can't teach suspended children who are not in school, but we shouldn't warehouse or "babysit" students who continuously infringe on the rights of others or prevent teaching staff from their primary duty of teaching and motivating the vast majority of their students who are compliant and want to learn.

A positive learning environment encourages imagination, "fun" learning, and enhances the unique, individual development of each child. In contrast, negative environments cause teachers to get out of the profession not because of teaching, but because of lack of administrative/parental support. It's called professional "burnout" and many districts lose half their initially hired teachers in five to seven years discounting factors such as retirement, family moves, or transfer for higher pay. We can't afford to lose the best of our teachers, especially in "high risk" schools whose students need them the most!

Note: Occasionally, every teacher will experience a class clown who feels it is his/her responsibility to entertain other students with humor and antagonize teachers with interruptions and colorful antics. If these are *positive* class clowns, a great teacher can guide and control their humor with reasonable parameters of mutual understanding and respect. Generally, positive clowns are very bright and need extra attention. Negative class clowns are mean-spirited and their intention is to ridicule, embarrass, and disrupt. This kind of conduct cannot be tolerated. For more insight and understanding, read William Watson Purkey's *Teaching Class Clowns (And What They Can Teach Us),* Corwin Press, 2006.

Chapter 13
Some Observations & Conclusions

There is no learning without obedience based on mutual respect, and there is no respectful obedience without discipline.

Discipline is an act of caring, which comes from the heart for the benefit of others. Whether it's a parent or educator disciplining a child or a drill instructor working with new recruits, it is always intended to make another person better than he/she is at the moment. Discipline must be reasonable, consistent, and take place in a structured environment with reasonable boundaries and consequences. Since discipline comes from within, it develops slowly and is motivated by love, not external force or a desire to dominate.

The hallmark of discipline is the positive development of *character*, which is the knowledge and inclination to do the right thing at the right time for the right reasons. It is the basis for compassion and altruism as well as empathy. *Leadership* is character in action for service to others before self.

In contrast to discipline, *punishment* is the use of *external* means to control someone through the use of consequences, which cause psychological or physical pain. Good behavior as a result of threatened punishment is not discipline, since it is merely behavior based on the *avoidance* of painful consequences. Discipline is always based on an *internal* compass of moral character, which is consistent no matter what the situational circumstances of supervision or no supervision.

If there are no consequences for inappropriate behavior, then negative behavior will persist. Motivating children to behave appropriately has better results if they *earn* what they want (rewards, positive reinforcement) rather than suffer the infliction of punishment (negative consequences). Sometimes, negative consequences that do not cause physical or emotional pain must be used before a child can internalize a sense of discipline. Good judgment and positive modification of behavior takes longer through age-appropriate discipline interventions than through the immediacy of punitive measures, which could cause resentment, anger, low self-esteem and actually engender more negative behavior.

The greatest *predictor* of a child becoming successful as a decent human being with good character is his/her *nuclear family* (mom, dad, siblings) with only rare exceptions. There are some individuals who overcame great environmental odds (dysfunctional family, poverty, neighborhoods of crime, and societal prejudice) to succeed, usually with one or more influential mentors (teachers, coaches, clergy, altruistic organizations).

Other than the nuclear family, the greatest influences on a child's future success as a decent human being is his/her neighborhood environment, school, peer group, and ultimately the child's attitude and willingness to participate, obey proper authority, work hard, and persevere toward the attainment of worthy goals which create positive self-esteem (respect for self and others).

Less than 14 percent of a child's waking hours are spent on academic development in schools (see chapter 8), so it is ludicrous to hold schools totally accountable for the total success of children in personal and cognitive development. Educators do not control the other 86 percent of a child's life, which directly influences a child's motivation to succeed. Obviously, we occasionally read about academically successful, "high risk" schools despite negative environmental odds. However, the *sustainability* of this success for over ten or twenty years is dependent on maintaining the same leadership with little or no staff turnover. Plus, one size does not fit all since replication of successful programs often don't work in other school districts. The combination of variables is infinite and unique for every school.

Good judgment comes from experience and experience comes from poor judgment. This is not failure unless repeated, which means no learning has taken place for positive growth. Failure occurs only when one stops trying. Again, hard work and *perseverance* (never giving up) in the pursuit of worthy goals is another trait of good character.

Knowing when to accept, overcome, or adapt to uncontrollable life circumstances is resiliency and is a part of good judgment, an important trait parents and educators can teach children through the leadership of their own example. Everyone gets "knocked down" in life, but the *champions* always keep getting up and continue giving their best! You can outscore champions but you can never beat 'em!

When parents and teachers *allow* children to make mistakes (not life threatening), they hold children accountable for dealing with the outcomes. This is sometimes called "tough love," but is also an act of discipline to teach *resiliency* and internalize good judgment. Over-protective parents or educators who try to insulate children from reality are unwittingly enabling children *not* to be accountable for their mistakes and actually promote an attitude of entitlement or hollow expectation by some children that someone will always "bail them out" or help them cover up their mistakes.

In a home, school, or society, when anything goes, everything goes. If there are no standards of conduct (civility, dress, manners, respect, self-control, etc.) then the result is the unpredictability of chaos and dysfunction because everyone "does his/her own thing." High expectations for standards of behavior do not inhibit individuality. Parameters and boundaries within a structured environment can be wide enough to encourage individual choices within those parameters. In short, every team has an individual style in how they execute their plays but within the parameters of the rules and regulations governing the sport.

Since there is no single *manual* for parenting or educating children, always let love be your guide to age-appropriate discipline strategies, which will be effective in growing successful adults for the future. The answers are not in curriculum guides, standard courses of study, benchmark testing for growth, spreadsheets of curriculum alignment, or all the university methods courses for teaching. Nor are the answers in parenting "how to" books or "self-help" books on being a better person. The answer is unique within each one of us, yet universal as indicated by the common thread which runs through all the great tenets, lessons, and wonderful books of all the major religions of the world. If each one of us always acts with the *intentionality to do good and help others* by putting service before self, we could co-exist in collective peace and individual fulfillment. Any scripture is easy to read and easy to believe. The hard part is *living our scriptures* and truly *listening* to our hearts where God's intentionality for us is always spoken.

Appendices

The intent of the following appendices is to serve as an adjunct to *Care Enough to Discipline*. They are illustrations of the philosophy and values that enhance universal and positive character traits regardless of race, gender, or socioeconomic status. If parents and educators fail to work together in raising children for the global village of the 21st century and *be the examples they want their children to become*, then we will keep producing adults who are spiritually bankrupt. Their dysfunctional behaviors toward self-centered, negative ends will continue to wreak havoc and chaos in all global societies. For several decades, there has been more per capita expenditure in arresting, trying, and incarcerating these kinds of individuals (criminals, gang members, terrorists) than we appropriate in school budgets to educate each child. Again, these appendices are simply a loose collection of "stuff" I have saved over the years and I hope they will inspire you, as they have inspired me, to do the right thing for our children.

—Dr. Lane Anderson (Dr. "A")

Note: If you have teenage children and this guide fails to be effective, simply post the notice below on the refrigerator door where they will be sure to see it.

CHILDREN
Tired of being harassed
by your stupid parents?
ACT NOW!
Move out, get a job,
and pay your own bills,
while you still know everything!

—Anonymous

APPENDIX A
OUR ATTITUDE IS OUR ALTITUDE IN LIFE

The following assertions illustrate this simple fact of life:

Think Positive
If you think you are beaten, you are.
If you think you dare not, you won't.
Success begins with your own will . . .
It's all your state of mind.
Life's battles are not always won by those who are
stronger or faster;
Sooner or later the person who wins is the person
who thinks he can.
—ANONYMOUS

"The longer I live, the more I realize the impact of attitude on life. Attitude, to me, is more important than facts. It is more important than the past, than education, than money, than circumstances, than failures, than successes, than what other people think or say or do. It is more important than appearance, giftedness or skill. It will make or break a company, a church, a home.

The remarkable thing is we have a choice every day regarding the attitude we will embrace for that day. We cannot change our past . . . we cannot change the fact that people will act in a certain way. We cannot change the inevitable. The only thing we can do is play on the one thing we have, and that is our attitude . . .

I am convinced that life is 10% what happens to me and 90% how I react to it. And so it is with you . . . we are in charge of our Attitudes."

—CHARLES SWINDOLL,
Evangelical Christian Pastor, Author, Educator,
Founder of Insight for Living
Plano, Texas

Attitude often determines your altitude in life. It is one of the greatest attributes parents and educators can instill within all our children from living their own lives with faith, courage, discipline, and positive actions to overcome life's challenges.
—L.S.A.

APPENDIX B
WHAT EVERY CHILD NEEDS

Fun. Take time to laugh and play and share the wonders of life with me.

Affection. Warm hugs will nurture me and make this world a much friendlier place.

Acceptance. Appreciate me for the individual I am, with all my unique gifts and special talents.

Respect. Treat me like an important and valuable person, and I'll learn to respect and honor myself and others.

Praise. Tell me all the things you appreciate about me so I'll know how wonderful I really am.

Security. Give me boundaries that will allow me to grow safely, feel secure, and overcome my fears.

Honesty. Share your real feelings and admit your mistakes to me, so I'll learn what it means to be a whole person.

Patience. Be understanding when I make my own mistakes; and remember—even when it doesn't seem like it, I'm trying my best.

Forgiveness. Remind me that nobody's perfect, and that it feels much better to forgive than to hold a grudge.

Encouragement. Support me and be positive as I try new things, and I'll have the courage to keep exploring.

Openness. Listen to me, and be open to what you may be able to learn from me.

Love. If you care for me in all these ways, you will be giving me the best life has to offer.

—Anonymous

Appendix C
Some Characteristics Common to Effective Leaders

I wrote the following definitions primarily for business and industry settings, but they are also applicable to parents, teachers, and school administrators. It is by no means comprehensive as there have been many books written on leadership. These are more like "bullet statements" rather than complete sentences and are based on experience and observation, not an exhaustive research of "the literature." Hopefully, my readers will internalize most of the statements through personal affirmation of what they already know and are practicing.

Integrity: trustworthy, dependable, honest, open and direct communication.

Trust: believe the "best" in others until proven otherwise, positive assumptions about others as being able, valuable, and responsible. Empower people, do not micromanage.

Delegation of Authority: based on mutual trust with subordinates in "getting the job done" through shared authority/decision-making. Understand that one can delegate authority but never responsibility. The key is to become "dispensable" not indispensable in creating team competence.

Humility: never arrogant or rude due to positional authority or advanced training/competence. Do not have to "pull rank" to get things done (except in unique or extreme circumstances). Realizes that some subordinates have superior knowledge in selective areas of operational competence and values it. Asks input/opinion from others as appropriate.

Communication: very effective in sending and receiving information both verbally and in writing. Good listener and knows how to "disagree agreeably". Strong ability to influence and persuade others to work as a team or family unit. Very open and does not gossip, start rumors, or betray confidentiality.

Respect: maintains positive self-esteem through respect for "self" (non-conceit or self-admiration) and for others even if they don't deserve it.

Self-Control: maintains composure and calm demeanor, even during tough times or situations of high stress caused by unreasonable organizational demands, client expectations, or conflict within the team, family, or company. Grace under pressure is always reassuring to subordinates.

Mediator: understanding multiple points of view (diversity) and how to integrate these perceptions into a unified whole through collaboration and consensus toward mutual goals and objectives.

Energy: must be in good health with good stress management skills and maintain a reasonable balance between work and personal life.

Compassion: maintains empathy for others for better understanding of internal motivation of significant others and subordinates. Knows each of his/her significant others or staff personally without being intrusive or allowing personal situations to negatively influence professional, parental, or teacher expectations.

Optimism: when things break down or go wrong, or when there are seemingly insurmountable obstacles, these situations are simply perceived as "challenges" which can be overcome. Believes that there is room for improvement and that things will get better every day. Continuous positive attitude.

Confidence: strong belief in capabilities of "self" (again without conceit or arrogance) regardless of outside antagonism or criticism. Also unwavering belief in the competency and capability of his/her significant others or staff while always conveying a tone of mutual respect and trust.

Commitment: ensures that the entire team remains focused (mission/vision) and unified toward achieving company goals of productivity and quality control with on-time delivery of goods or services and within corporate guidelines and policy. Is able to continuously sustain motivation of 100 percent effort every day within both himself/herself and subordinates. Parents do this for their families based on core values and positive character development.

Motivator: closely tied in with commitment as already stated. If a leader is not motivated by positive family/professional ideals, how can he/she motivate others in this regard? Continuously instills a sense of purpose and meaning in the accomplishment and pride in a job well done.

Positive attitude: understands that one's *attitude* is his/her *altitude* in approaching work and life. Must always be "up" even when feeling "down" as an example for others to emulate and follow. "Every day is a good day" at XYZ company, school, or family.

Passion: must be motivated by an inner passion (drive or "juice") and belief in what they do, how they live, and why.

Strives to get better every day. Has the ability to instill this feeling in children and staff so there is more joy in family/school environments and team accomplishments.

Competence: must have demonstrated a high level of job performance-related competence in addition to effective "people skills" so there is a common perception that he/she worked hard to "earn" higher positional authority rather than by "political" appointment. In a family sense, parents follow their hearts and care enough to discipline.

Decisive: allows and encourages multiple inputs, but is able to come to a decisive conclusion for action and implementation. Does not "waffle" or become "wishy-washy" as situations change. Parents and educators must be consistent in working with children and staff. Consistency is the hallmark of fairness.

Flexibility: while being decisive and maintaining a steady course of action, he/she must be *receptive to new information,* which might require a course of action change. A stubborn "my way or the highway" attitude or tight-fisted centralized control ("nothing moves without my signature") shows insecurity and defensiveness. It will also stifle children's and staff creativity and input.

Management: must be able to align *action* of staff members with organizational *written* policies, regulations, and procedures. Again, must set the example to maximize results. This is true for families, which must live within structured boundaries, rules, and consistent consequences.

Character: doing the right thing at the right time for the right reasons. Strong conviction in core values regardless of situations, politics or expediency. Opposite of self-centeredness or self-promotion. Very much oriented and motivated toward service to others, team, company, or family.

Recognition: encourages and gives credit to others for family/staff success (never self). If the team is not successful in any aspect of product or service, he/she always takes the "heat" and does not blame individuals or the team. "The buck stops here." Praises team members (or team) in public and *constructively* criticizes individuals in private. This is true for families as the parents are always responsible for their children taking accountability for individual actions.

Counseling: if mutual trust is established for confidentiality, he/she is always available to listen to a team member's personal/family problems, especially if situations are affecting work performance. Knowing a team leader/supervisor understands is an emotional morale booster and reduces absenteeism. When parents actively listen to their children, the bond of trust and flow of respectful communication increases and alienation and dysfunctional behavior decreases.

Sense of humor: always take your job seriously but not yourself. *Appropriate* humor at work or home relieves staff/family stress and anxiety and improves morale. When parents do this, children feel more secure and perceive their parents as caring and not rigidly stern.

Loyalty: except in rare instances of illegal activity or violation of company policy or regulations, always "back" your people. Loyalty works up and *down* the chain of command. Parents must trust the judgment of educators regarding their children, but also be supportive of each child trying to learn from wrong choices.

Leadership: the consistent belief in and practice of all the aforementioned traits. Must have the ability to "read" change in situational variables during fluid circumstances caused by internal/external stressors and apply the appropriate leadership/managerial style to maintain positive results or resolution of problems. Must never forget that one manages things but leads people. Must know his/her people, job, and self to lead by example (i.e. "walk the talk"). Parenting is the most difficult leadership position in any society. Parents must always be the example of what they want their children to become in life.

Note: Ironically, family members treat each other worse than they do others outside the family environment. Of course, there is a practical reason for this, as students can be suspended or adults fired if they are disobedient, disrespectful, or disruptive in school or business settings. However, any person of character will do his/her best to act in a positive manner in *any* environment.

Appendix D
Some Thoughts on Children
and Schooling

Compiled by Dr. Lane S. Anderson (Dr. "A")

On the very few days I experienced overwhelming odds, indifference, or stress (like anyone else who is passionate about what they do in life to serve others), the following is what I would pull out of my briefcase and read. This process would re-center my soul with a reminder of what my meaning and purpose was despite bureaucratic constraints and unreasonable people. In minutes, I would feel re-energized with the idealism, energy, and focus toward what I was "called" to do for children and families. I hope you will also feel somewhat the same after reading over these philosophical excerpts, most by people far more talented than I, for your own inspiration.

> *Every child can learn (and should learn) to the best of his ability. Our job as educators is to provide the conditions for success to happen every day for every child. Success is the "Breakfast of Champions."*
>
> —Dr. "A"

> *The secret of education lies in respecting the pupil.*
> —Emerson

Our children need our love and support. Even though they may give up on themselves, we must never give up on them . . . To do so is educationally dangerous and morally unforgivable.

> —George McKenna, past principal of George Washington Preparatory High School, Los Angeles, CA

We can, whenever and wherever we choose, successfully teach all children whose schooling is of interest to us. We already know more than we need to know to do that. Whether or not we do it must finally depend on how we feel about the fact that we haven't so far.

> —Ron Edmonds on "Effective Schools"

If a child does not learn from the way we teach, then we will teach him the way he learns.

> —Rita Dunn

Nobody cares how much you know until they know how much you care.

> —William W. Purkey

The most important thing we can teach children is courage; first and foremost, courage to believe in themselves; courage to stand up for and persist in the achievement of worthy ideals no matter what the odds. If we succeed in teaching nurturing, and sustaining this one facet of character, children's academic competence, compassion, confidence, and commitment will naturally follow.

> —Dr. "A"

Human potential, though not always apparent, is there waiting to be discovered and invited forth.
—WILLIAM W. PURKEY, International Alliance for Invitational Education

Every child is gifted and talented, disadvantaged and at risk, to some degree. Our mission as educators is to enhance the former and diminish the latter.
—DR. "A"

The end of "training" is to learn something specific but the end of "education" is to learn how to learn; without this, all training is futile; for the knowledge and aptitudes needed in one decade become nearly obsolete in the next.
—SYDNEY HARRIS

Our aim is still for our school to be the best. What that means to me is a school without failure where all children leave school having identified a talent, a skill, an intelligence through which they can become whatever they want to be.
—MICHAEL ALEXANDER, *Principal,* Simon Guggenheim School, New York

A principal should be both an instructional leader and a management facilitator while never forgetting that one leads people and manages things. The principal is the catalyst of positive change and sustainer of a common vision in providing an "inviting" climate for effective teaching and learning for all children.
—DR. "A"

Beauty is not seen with the eye but with the soul, and every child is beautiful.

—ANONYMOUS

In a completely rational society, the best of us would aspire to be teachers and the rest of us would have to settle for something less, because passing civilization along from one generation to the next ought to be the highest honor and the highest responsibility anyone could have.

—LEE IACOCCA
Former Chrysler Chairman

Educating the mind without educating the heart is no education at all.

—ARISTOTLE

School success is a lot like democracy: it cannot be mandated or imposed. It is the product of people working together in a representative, fair, and cooperative way.

—JAMES P. COMER,
School Power, 1980

Schools must become caring moral communities that help children from unhappy homes focus on their work, control their anger, feel cared about, and become responsible students.

—THOMAS LICKOMA,
The Return of Character Education, 1991

I am only one, but I am one. I cannot do everything, but I can do something; and that I should do and can do, by the grace of God I will do.

—THELMA HAMMONDS HUGGINS, Lumbee

Reading is to the mind what exercise is to the body.
—SIR RICHARD STEELE

A hundred years from now it will not matter what my bank account was, the type of house I lived in, or the kind of car I drove—but the world may be different because I was important in the life of a child.
—ANONYMOUS

A good school is like a good family. The cornerstone is absolute trust among all its members followed by open communication, respect, and a unified commitment toward the common good of others through selfless teamwork. The result is the development of good character in young people who constantly experience adult role models of compassion, courage, self-discipline, and unconditional love. When good families and good schools work together, students naturally become successful, confident, and caring citizens of tomorrow.
—DR. "A"

APPENDIX E
SOME SUGGESTIONS WHICH VIRTUALLY GUARANTEE THAT ANYONE CAN AVOID LONG-TERM POVERTY IN AMERICA

Walter E. Williams is a black professor of economics at George Mason University just outside Washington, DC. Now in his early seventies, he grew up in pre-civil rights America and knows what it is like to live with racial injustice, prejudice, and discrimination. Yet, many of his syndicated newspaper columns discount these past experiences as excuses for not taking responsibility and accountability for one's preparation for competition in life. An excerpt from one of his 2005 columns* serves as a summary of this assertion as follows: "Avoiding long-term poverty is not rocket science. First, graduate from high school. Second, get married before you have children, and stay married. Third, work at any kind of job, even one that starts out paying the minimum wage. And finally, avoid engaging in criminal behavior."

Williams goes on to say that graduating with a B or C average will often mean availability of financial assistance for post-high school training. Also, if a husband and wife both earn minimum wages, their combined incomes would exceed $21,000, almost $3,000 above the poverty line of $18,810 for a family of four (U.S. Bureau of Census, 2003). He also contends that racial discrimination does not prevent any student from paying attention in class, studying, or completing high school. Williams does not see racial discrimination as the cause for a high rate of black, single parent households or disproportionate school dropout rates for black students. "Is it racial discrimination that's responsible for the 68 percent illegitimacy rate among blacks?"

Williams goes on to point out that most black, two parent households who have managed to live by the aforementioned guidelines, have definitely avoided poverty. " . . . Among black households that included a married couple, over 50 percent were middle class earning above $50,000 and 26 percent earned more than $75,000 (1999 Bureau of Census Report). How in the world did these black families manage not to be poor? Did America's racists cut them some slack?"

In essence, Williams seems to encourage anyone, regardless of race or socioeconomic level, to become proactive in overcoming any barrier in life and not become a passive, or angry, blaming victim of any person, institution, policy, procedure, regulation, or the history of past events.

However, being proactive and individually responsible/accountable for one's life requires character, determination, hard work, and perseverance in the pursuit of one's goals and dreams. This kind of positive development can begin early in all children's lives if they have the continuous, positive guidance and adult role modeling of caring parents and educators, as well as supportive communities who all care enough to discipline.

*Quotes are from his nationally syndicated column appearing in the *Times-News*, Burlington, NC: "Three Basic Tips on How Not to be Poor," published on May 13, 2005.

Editorial Note: While Dr. Williams uses his own race as an *example* of how not to be poor, in this column his assertions are *generic to all people* who do not live responsibly with a sense of accountability for their actions. In essence, it's about developing the character of maturity through discipline, self-control, hard work, and compassion for others regardless of race, ethnic heritage, or gender. Dr. King said it best in his 1963 "I Have a Dream" speech:

In the process of gaining our rightful place we must not be guilty of wrongful deeds . . . Let us not satisfy our thirst for freedom by drinking from the cup of bitterness and hatred. We must forever conduct our struggle on the high plain of dignity and discipline. We must not allow our creative protest to generate into physical violence. Again and again we must rise to the majestic heights of meeting physical force with soul force . . . I have a dream my four little children will one day live in a nation where they will not be judged by the color of their skin but by the content of their character . . .

—Dr. Martin Luther King, Jr.

Editorial Note: In my opinion, Barack and Michelle Obama represent one of the best examples of what Professor Williams means by being proactive in one's life despite seemingly humble beginnings. The Obamas' parallel visions and work, perseverance, discipline, and courage in living are the essence of Dr. King's dream, unlimited in their respective individual achievements as successful, caring adults.

Observation: My dad, Lane Anderson, Jr., was a deacon in a church in Charlotte, NC in the late 1950s. In a board of deacons meeting, there was a decision made to seat "people of color" on the back row, should they decide to attend our church services. My dad made it known that any of God's children could sit anywhere in the "Lord's House" as they wished, then promptly resigned.

Personal Note: Some of my dad's "isms" that he taught me in my teen years with regard to character, discipline, and self-reliance would probably be agreeable to Walter Williams' philosophy:

- Observation, not old age, brings wisdom.
- Overcoming adversity is the greatest teacher of character.
- Any boy can make a baby. It takes a man to raise one.
- Any boy can get drunk. It takes a man to stay in control, no matter what he drinks.
- Almost everyone is racist to some degree, whether subconsciously or intentionally. Never be prejudiced toward anyone, but *discrimination* for personal association purposes is fine *after* observing another person's behavior and intentions. Beware of anyone acting like "the victim" due to historical events you did not create or, to "blame' you through verbal or written attempts to manipulate you by inflicting a sense of guilt.

I have learned that success is to be measured not so much by the position that one has reached in life as by the obstacles which one has overcome while trying to succeed.
—Booker T. Washington

APPENDIX F
FIVE PREMISES OF LIFE

Everyone has a different set of core values, which evolve from childhood, are based on faith, and finally, life experiences. It has been my observation as both an educator and parent that children who are raised with the character-building traits as mentioned in this guide are much more confident, self-reliant, compassionate, courageous, and resilient in adapting to life's problems, hardships, and tragedies.

Family members and great teachers who are positive role models always teach children through their *example* regardless of economic circumstances, race, or gender. Accepting the following five premises of life as part of one's core values will go a long way in *preventing* children from becoming adults who feel like victims or blame others for their circumstances by expressing frequent anger toward people or institutions. They will also learn to avoid internalizing guilt from others and avoid manipulating others through negative comments or guilt (especially from events of the past). Negative people generally choose their own misery while also attempting to suck the life out of others through their constant aura of pessimistic attitude, insecurities, and low self-esteem. These are people who can destroy a family, sometimes commit crimes, and generally create chaos and dysfunction wherever they go. Children who grow up internalizing the following premises as part of their core values will become optimistic, proactive in creating their own destiny, and become assets to their families and humanity in general.

- Life is not always *fair.*
- Nobody *owes* you anything.
- You cannot always control what happens to *you* in life, but you can control *your reaction* to it.
- You are ultimately *accountable* and *responsible* for your own *happiness.*
- Other than survival, the greatest need in life is *to love and be loved unconditionally* through faith and/or relationships with significant others.

Of course, this list in not definitive or meant to be a formula for living. Any reader can certainly add his/her own premises or axioms, but raising children to become successful human beings is dependent on exposure to positive role models who have character, self-discipline, compassion, courage, a good work ethic, high self-esteem, and perseverance, which teaches children that *they never fail until they stop trying.*

Imagine life as a game in which you are juggling some five balls in the air. You name them work, family, health, friends, and spirit—and you're keeping all of these in the air. You will soon understand that "work" is a rubber ball. If you drop it, it will bounce back. But the other four balls—family, health, friends, and spirit—are made of glass. If you drop one of these, they will be irrevocably scuffed, marked, nicked, damaged, or even shattered. They will never be the same . . . Yesterday is history. Tomorrow is a mystery. Today is a gift: that's why we call it "the present."

—BRIAN DYSON, Past CEO, Coca-Cola Co.
From " A Life of Balance"

APPENDIX G
REAL LOVE BEGINS WITH YOURSELF

Parents and educators who raise children with unconditional love, acceptance of their unique giftedness, who give their time for meaningful interaction, and who care enough to discipline will create adults who are empowered with a strong self-esteem to make good judgments and choices throughout life. This does not mean a self-esteem based on selfishness, arrogance, conceit, or greed. Rather, it is a self-concept based on positive universal values and having an optimistic attitude in addition to the confidence and sense of empowerment to be proactive (refusing to be a victim) in living the destiny of one's dreams which give positive meaning and purpose to life.

If you can't love yourself in this manner, you can't truly give or receive authentic love. Raising children to believe in themselves is illustrated in the following words of self-reflection (anyone may insert his/her name in the beginning statement):

I am _____ (your name). I am able, valuable, and responsible, unique and special. Though I need to give and receive love, I know that I must *first* love myself as a creation of God with gifts and talents that can help others. This lends purpose to life and makes each day meaningful.

When I learn to love myself, it is an affirmation and

an approximation of God's perfect love on earth. This inner knowledge gives me strength to love others unconditionally as well as to practice forgiveness. No one has the right to judge, criticize, or diminish who I am inside. It is the soul of my personhood, which I can protect by *choosing* what to internalize and what to reject. I refuse to be a victim of anyone's comments, perceptions, or actions. Ultimately, I am responsible and accountable for my own happiness in life realizing that others can only *enrich* the quality of my life experience.

I must understand that while I cannot always control what happens to me in this life, I can *control* my reaction to life's events and circumstances. To blame others for my condition in life is to become a victim. Only I can *choose* not to be a victim or to be manipulated by shame or guilt inflicted by others.

I will trust and follow my heart in being compassionate toward others in general and selectively love those who are closest to me. If my love is rejected or not returned in a sustained commitment, I must have the courage to redirect this very personal gift from my soul. True, unconditional love must be reciprocal or it will die. I cannot make others love me nor can I act the pretense of loving others if it is not true. Authentic love is given freely from the spiritual self and is returned if it is meant to be. Loving God is the first and greatest law of life, which enables me to truly love others as myself. This is the universal essence of all religions and the key to achieving inner contentment, happiness, and world peace.

—Dr. Lane S. Anderson
The Anderson Center for Marriage and Family Therapy

All love is based on caring emotion, and the character and self-discipline to put others before one's self. One of the best, comprehensive definitions of love which is applicable to relationships in families, schools, and between individuals is from *The Holy Bible*:

Love
Love is patient and kind;
love is not jealous or boastful;
it is not arrogant or rude.
Love does not insist on its own way;
it is not irritable or resentful;
it does not rejoice at wrong,
but rejoices in the right.
Love bears all things,
believes all things,
hopes all things,
endures all things.
Love never ends.
—I CORINTHIANS 13: 4-8

And again from *The Little Prince*:

*It is only with the heart that one can see rightly;
what is essential is invisible to the eye.*
—ANTOINE DE SAINT-EXUPERY

APPENDIX H
TWO PROFILES IN COURAGE

Overcoming adversity in life through hard work, perseverance, courage, and a passion to live one's dreams takes exceptional discipline and builds character, confidence, good judgment, and self-esteem. The following are two examples of what *Care Enough to Discipline* is all about.

> *He cannot make a fist. The right wrist's motion is limited to 40 percent. The little finger on the left hand is numb, partially paralyzed and scarred from a childhood accident. The joints of the other nine fingers are fused. There is mobility in only one distal joint, that of the middle finger of the left hand. These are the hands of Byron Janis, who today is acclaimed as one of the world's great piano virtuosos.*
> —"To Conquer Fear," *Parade Magazine*, 1985

Kyle Maynard was born with a rare disorder called congenital amputation, which means that he has no forearms, shortened legs with no feet, and he stands about four feet tall. Despite daily challenges, Kyle is an excellent student, has beautiful writing skills, and can type 50 words per minute. Kyle's competitive spirit, determination, character and work ethic enabled him to become one of the top high school wrestlers in Georgia. He also broke the world record in the modified bench press by lifting 360 pounds, over three times his body weight. Kyle went on to enjoy much success at the University of Georgia. In 2005, he wrote a book about his experiences called *No Excuses* (Regency Publishing, 2005).

Appendix I
The Inspiration of Gratitude

Too often in life, we take for granted all the blessings we have received over the years and focus only on what is unfair, life's disappointments, or all the "things" we don't have. The following words should be an inspiration for not only educators of children but also parents and anyone else who, by the grace of God, have the ability to rise each morning and go forth in service to others.

Thank You Lord

Even though I clutch my blanket and growl when the alarm clock rings each morning, Thank you, Lord, that I can hear. There are those who are deaf.

Even though I keep my eyes tightly closed, against the morning light as long as possible, Thank you, Lord, that I can see. There are those that are blind.

Even though I huddle in my bed and put off the physical effort of rising, Thank you, Lord, that I have the strength to rise. There are many who are bedfast.

Even though the first hour of my day is hectic, when socks are lost, toast is burned, tempers are short, Thank you, Lord, for my family.

And even though our breakfast table never looks like the pictures in the magazine and the menu is at times unbalanced, Thank you, Lord, for the food we have. There are so many who are hungry.

Even though the routine of my job is challenging, Thank you, Lord, for the opportunity to work. There are many who have no job.

Even though I grumble and bemoan my faith from day to day, and wish my circumstances were not so modest, Thank you, Lord, for the gift of life.

And even though I work in a profession that does not get the support from society that it richly deserves, I don't make the salary of a professional athlete, I don't enjoy the prestige of a doctor or lawyer, and I don't receive the hero-worship of an entertainer, Thank you, Lord, for giving me the opportunity to finish your magnificent work by being a positive force in the lives of children made in your image.

Thank you for giving me a touch of the divine.

—Dr. Edward Joyner, et.al,
Former Executive Director, Comer School
Development Program, Yale University

Note: Dr. Joyner is currently Professor of Education at Sacred Heart University in Trumbull, CT. He can be reached by email at *joynere1200@sacredheart.edu.*

SYNTHESIS

Hopefully, each reader of this guide has derived some benefit with regard to raising children for the 21st century through caring enough to discipline. Educating everyone takes everyone in the community of humankind regardless of race, ethnic origin, gender, title, nationality, or socioeconomic status. Every human being is consciously or unconsciously a teacher for someone else through the leadership of living a positive life. All adults are parents for all our children regardless of biological connection. We are a global family.

Whether children are in school, in their family home, out in their general community, or in a place of worship, there can be no learning without obedience, and there is no obedience without discipline. Positive, fair, and reasonable discipline is an act of love and caring. When any adult in a child's life acts with the maturity of self-control, courage, compassion, respect, tolerance, a strong work ethic, and the perseverance to pursue positive outcomes and dreams in life, he/she is teaching by more than words or books can convey. Again, Margaret Mead reminds us: "The solution of adult problems tomorrow depends in large measure upon the way our children grow up today. There is no greater insight into the future than recognizing that when we save our children—we save ourselves."

—L.S.A.

The ability to show love must always be part of the human equation. Technology has not crossed that barrier. The day love dies will be the virtual end of the world.
—STEVEN SPIELBERG, *Reader's Digest,* August 2005

It is we who have to be His love, His compassion in the world of today. But to be able to love we must have faith, for faith in action is love, and love in action is service.
—MOTHER THERESA, *Mother Theresa: Come Be My Light,* edited by Brian Kolodiejchuk, M.C.

If we don't change, we don't grow. If we don't grow, we aren't really living.
—GAIL SHEEHY, *Author*

But the fruit of the Spirit is love, joy, peace, patience, kindness, goodness, faithfulness, gentleness, and self-control.
—Galatians 5:22

We make a living by what we get. We make a life by what we give.
—SIR WINSTON CHURCHILL

No one grows old by living, only by losing interest in living.
—MARIE BEYNON RAY

Life isn't about waiting for the storm to pass. It's about learning to dance in the rain.
—ANONYMOUS

ABOUT THE AUTHOR

Dr. Anderson completed his undergraduate and master's degrees at the University of North Carolina at Chapel Hill and a doctorate in educational administration and leadership at the University of North Carolina at Greensboro. He also completed four years of post-doctoral work in the field of human development and family studies.

Dr. Anderson was an educator for 33 years with eleven years teaching/coaching experience in grades 5-12 and specialized in teaching the American novel and composition at the high school level. He was principal of two elementary schools and one middle school, all of which were known for high student achievement, closing minority achievement gaps, strong parental support, and excellent school-wide discipline. Additionally, he was the principal of five successful summer school programs for inner city, high-risk students and students with severe disabilities. Before entering the field of education, Dr. Anderson served for four years on active duty in the United States Navy on both surface warfare and amphibious assault ships. He also served for 21 years in the naval reserve intelligence program, retiring with the rank of captain.

Dr. Anderson is a frequent presenter at local, state, and international conferences on a variety of educational topics such as school-wide discipline, classroom management, character development, closing minority achievement gaps, and leadership. Dr. Anderson received the Wachovia Principal of the Year Award in Guilford County, N.C. (127 schools). He was also selected as North Carolina's Principal of the Year, and designated a National Distinguished Principal by the US Department of Education and the National Association of Elementary (K-8) School Principals (NAESP). He received the Patrick Francis Daly Memorial Award for Excellence in Educational Leadership from the Comer School Development Program at Yale University. Dr. Anderson was also recognized by the graduate schools of education at UNC-Chapel Hill and UNC-Greensboro for the Alumni Achievement and Distinguished Career Awards respectively. He has published several articles on effective teaching and motivating high-risk students in various educational journals.

Dr. Anderson is a Board Certified Clinical Member of the American Association for Marriage and Family Therapy (AAMFT) and continues his private practice of over 18 years along with his *Real World Consulting* business, which specializes in helping high-risk schools. He writes a monthly column on relationships called "Ask Dr. A" for *Alamance Magazine*. Dr. Anderson continues to teach in the Business and Industry Training Program at Alamance Community College near Mebane, where he lives with his wife "Charlie."

Contact Information

Dr. Lane Anderson, president of *Real World Consulting* specializes in working with high-risk schools that want to improve. He can tailor staff development seminars to any K–12 school's needs after an on-site school visitation/observation for at least one full day. Dr. Anderson provides time-proven, no-cost, practitioner (real world) strategies, which increase student achievement, decrease student discipline problems, close minority achievement gaps, produce supportive parents, and create a sense of purpose and teamwork among professional staff toward unified goals and objectives. Also, he helps K–12 schools establish Centers for Academic and Reflective Education (CARE) which are guaranteed to reduce out-of-classroom referrals by at least 40% in the first semester. He can be contacted at:

Real World Consulting
P.O. Box 798, Mebane, NC 27302
Phone: (919) 563-5050 Fax: (919) 563-2997
Email: *realworld@triad.rr.com*
Website: *www.careenoughtodiscipline.com*

Additionally, Dr. Anderson recommends the consulting/training services of the contacts on the following pages for selective staff development by specialists in the areas noted in bold headings:

Character Education
E. Perry Good, Consultant
Connected Schools
New View Publications
P.O. Box 3021, Chapel Hill, NC 27515-3021
(800) 441-3604 Fax: (919) 942-3760
www.NewViewPublications.com

Jon Oliver, Consultant
Lesson One: The ABC's of Life
The Lesson One Foundation, Inc.
245 Newbury Street, Room 2F, Boston, MA 02117
(617) 247-2787 Fax: (617) 247-3462
www.LessonOne.org

Philip F. Vincent, Consultant
Character Development Group, Inc.
P.O. Box 9211,Chapel Hill, NC 27515-9211
(919) 967-2110 Fax: (919) 967-2139
www.CharacterEducation.com

Comer School Development Program
School Development Program
Yale Child Study Center
55 College Street, New Haven, CT 06510-3208
(203) 737-1020 Fax: (203) 737-4001
www.SchoolDevelopmentProgram.org

Effective Schools
Dr. Larry Lezotte, Education Consultant
Effective Schools Products, Ltd.
Dept. F02, 2199 Jolly Road, Suite 160
Okemos, MI 48864
(700) 827-8041 Fax: (517) 349-8852
www.EffectiveSchools.com

Effective Teaching
Harry K. Wong and Rosemary T. Wong
Harry K. Wong Publications, Inc.
943 North Shoreline Blvd.
Mountain View, CA 94043
(650) 965-7896 Fax: (650) 965-7890
www.EffectiveTeaching.com

International Alliance for Invitational Education
Dr. William Watson Purkey
Director, NC Center for Invitational Education
4407 Williamsburg Road
Greensboro, NC 27410
(336) 855-7034 Fax: (336) 634-2496
www.purkey@aol.com

Jack Shmidt, Ed.D.
Executive Director, International Alliance for Invitational Education
Mail Drop 9106
Town Point Building
1000 Chastain Road
Kennesaw, GA 30144
(336) 363-9591
iaie@invitationaleducation.net

International Alliance for Invitational Education
PO Box 5173
Marietta, GA 30061-5173
(770) 422-9474
www.InvitationalEducation.net

PAIDEIA
National Paideia Center
400 Silver Cedar Court, Suite 200
Chapel Hill, NC 27514
(919) 962-3128 Fax: (919) 962-3139
www.Paideia.org

Association for Psychological Type (APT)
Experts in Jungian psychology and the administration/interpretation of the Myers-Briggs Type Indicator© (MBTI), the most widely used personality inventory in the world.

Mary Charles Blakebrough
APT Research Triangle Park
1431 Settlement Drive
Durham, NC 27713
Phone: (919) 493-5424
eFax: (919) 509-357-7510
mebreakthrough@mindspring.com
www.apt-nc.org

RECOMMENDED READING

Adler, Mortimer J. *The Paideia Proposal: An Educational Manifesto*. New York: Simon and Schuster, 1982.

Armstrong, Thomas. *Multiple Intelligences in the Classroom*. Alexandria, VA: Association for Supervision and Curriculum Development, 1994.

Ahrons, Constance. *We're Still Family: What Grown Up Children Say About Their Parents' Divorce*. New York: Harper Collins Publishers, 2004.

Angelou, Maya. *The Complete Collected Poems of Maya Angelou*. New York: Random House, 1994.

Bach, Richard. *Jonathan Livingston Seagull: A Story*. New York: The Macmillan Company, 1970.

Bauman, Lawrence. *The Nine Most Troublesome Teenage Problems and How to Solve Them*. New York: Ballantine Books, 1986.

Bolman, Lee G. and Terrence E. Deal. *Leading With Soul: An Uncommon Journey of Spirit*. San Francisco: Jossey-Bass Publishers, 1995.

Boteach, Shmuley. *Shalom in the Home: Smart Advice for a Peaceful Life*. Des Moines, Iowa: Meredith Books, 2007.

Brokaw, Tom. *The Greatest Generation*. New York: Random House, 1998.

Carson, Ben. *Think Big: Unleashing Your Potential for Excellence*. Grand Rapids, MI: Zondervan Publishing House, 1992.

Comer, James P. *Leave No Child Behind: Preparing Today's Youth for Tomorrow's World*. New Haven: Yale University Press, 2004.

—et al. *Rallying the Whole Village: The Comer Process for Rallying the Whole Village*. Columbia University: Teacher's College Press, 1996.

—*Waiting For A Miracle: Why Schools Can't Solve Our Problems—And How We Can*. New York: Penguin Putnam Inc, 1997.

Cosby, Bill and Alvin F. Poussaint. *Come On People: On the Path from Victims to Victors*. Nashville: Thomas Nelson Publishers, 2007.

Covey, Stephen R. *First Things First: To Live, to Love, to Learn, to Love, to Leave a Legacy*. New York: Free Press, 1994.

—*Principle-Centered Leadership*. New York: Simon and Schuster, 1990.

—*The Seven Habits of Highly Effective Families*. New York: Golden Books, 1997.

—*The Seven Habits of Highly Successful People*. New York: Free Press, 1989.

Davenport, Patricia and Gerald Anderson. *Closing the Achievement Gap: No Excuses*. Houston: The American Productivity and Quality Center, 2002.

Dixon, Steve. *Elementary School Guide to Character Education*. Chapel Hill, NC: Character Development Publishing, 2001.

Dryden, Gordon and Jeannette Vos. *The Learning Revolution*. Torrance, CA: Jalmar Press, 1994.

Dyer, Wayne W. *Being in Balance: 9 Principles for Creating*

Habits to Match Your Desires. New York: Hay House, Inc. 1996.

—*Excuses Be Gone! How to Change Lifelong, Self-Defeating Thinking Habits*. New York: Hay House, Inc. 2009.

—*The Power of Intention: Learning to Co-Create Your World Your Way*. New York: Hay House, Inc. 2004.

—*Wisdom of the Ages*. New York: Harper Collins, 1998.

Fisher, R. Stewart and Perry J. Martini. *Inspiring Leadership: Character and Ethics Matter*. Annapolis, MD: Academy Leadership Books, 2004.

Friedman, Thomas L. *The World Is Flat: A Brief History of the Twenty-First Century*. New York: Farrar, Strauss and Giroux, 2005.

Frankl, Victor. *Man's Search for Meaning*. Boston: Beacon Press, 1962.

Franklin, John Hope. *From Slavery to Freedom: A History of African Americans*. (2 vols. in 1). New York: Alfred A. Knopf, 2000.

Glasser, William. *Control Theory in the Classroom*. New York: Harper and Row, 1986.

—*Positive Addiction: How to Gain Strength and Self-Esteem Through Positive Power*. New York: Harper and Row Publishers, Inc, 1976.

—*The Quality School: Managing Students Without Coercion*. New York: Harper Perennial, 1990.

—*Schools Without Failure*. New York: Harper and Row, 1969.

Good, E. Perry, et al. *A Connected School*. Chapel Hill, NC: New View Publications, 2003.

Gray, John. *Children Are from Heaven: Positive Parenting Skills for Raising Cooperative, Confident, and Compassionate Children*. New York: Harper Collins Publishers, Inc., 1999.

Handbook of Research on Teaching: A Project of the American Educational Research Association. 3d ed. Edited by Merlin C. Wittrock. New York: Simon and Schuster MacMillan, 1986.

Harper, Hill. *Letters to a Young Brother: Manifest Your Destiny.* New York: Gotham Books, 2006.

Harrell, Keith. *Attitude Is Everything: 10 Life Changing Steps to Turning Attitude into Action.* New York: Harper Collins Publishers, 2003.

Harris, Alex and Brett. *Do Hard Things: A Teenage Rebellion Against Low Expectations.* Colorado Springs, CO: Multinomah Books, 2008.

Henderson, Jeff. *Cooked: My Journey From the Streets to the Stove.* New York: Harper Collins, 2008.

Hughes, Patrick Henry. *I Am Potential: Eight Lessons on Living, Loving, and Reaching Your Dreams.* Philadelphia: Da Capo Press Books, 2008.

Hurley, Bob, Sr., and Phil Pepe. *Divided Loyalties: The Diary of a Basketball Father.* New York: Pinnacle Books, 1993.

Jacobs, Jack and Douglas Century. *If Not Now, When?: Duty and Sacrifice in America's Time of Need.* New York: Penguin Group, 2008.

Jakes, T.D. *Reposition Yourself: Living Life Without Limits.* New York: Atria Books, 2007.

Jordan, Deloris. *Family First: Winning the Parenting Game.* San Francisco: Harper, 1996.

King, Martin Luther, Jr. *The Autobiography of Martin Luther King, Jr.* Edited by Clayborne Carson. New York: Warner Books, 1998.

—*I Have a Dream: Writings and Speeches that Changed the World.* Edited by James Melvin Washington. San Francisco: Harper Collins, 1986.

Leonard, George B. *Education and Ecstasy.* New York: Dell Co., Inc., 1968.

Lickona, Thomas. *Educating for Character: How Our Schools Can Teach Respect and Responsibility*. New York: Bantam Books, 1991.

Marx, Jeffrey. *Season of Life: A Football Star, a Boy, a Journey to Manhood*. New York: Simon & Schuster, 2003.

Maynard, Kyle. *No Excuses: The True Story of a Congenital Amputee Who Became a Champion in Wrestling and in Life*. Washington, D.C.: Regency Publishing, Inc, 2005.

McCloskey, Patrick J. *The Street Stops Here: A Year at a Catholic High School in Harlem*. Berkley: University of California Press, 2008.

McGraw, Phil. *Family First: Your Step-by-Step Plan for Creating a Phenomenal Family*. New York: Free Press, 2004.

—*Life Strategies: Doing What Works, Doing What Matters*. New York: Hyperion, 1999.

McGraw, Jay. *Life Strategies for Teens*. New York: Simon and Schuster, 2000.

Michener, James A. *The Quality of Life*. New York: J.B. Lippincott Co., 1970.

Mother Teresa: *Come Be My Light: The Private Writings of the "Saint of Calcutta."* Ed. Brian Kolodiejchuk. New York: Doubleday, 2007.

Murphy, Elizabeth. *The Developing Child: Using Jungian Type to Understand Children*. Mountain View, CA: Davies-Black Publishing, 1992.

Nader, Ralph. *The Seventeen Traditions*. New York: Harper Collins, 2007.

National Association of Elementary School Principals. *Leading Learning Communities: Standards for What Principals Should Know and Be Able to Do*. 2nd ed. Washington, DC: Collaborative Communications Group, 2008.

Nisbett, Richard E. *Intelligence and How to Get It: Why Schools and Cultures Count*. New York: W.W. Norton and Company, 2009.

Obama, Barack. *The Audacity of Hope: Thoughts on Reclaiming the American Dream*. New York: Three Rivers Press, 2006.

Oliver, Jon and Michael Ryan. *Lesson One: The ABC's of Life: The Skills We All Need But Were Never Taught*. New York: Simon and Schuster, 2004.

Palmer, Parker J. *The Courage to Teach: Exploring the Inner Landscape of a Teacher's Life*. San Francisco: Jossey-Bass Publishers, 1998.

Pausch, Randy with Jeffrey Zaslow. *The Last Lecture*. New York: Hyperion Books, 2008.

Purkey, William W. *Inviting School Success: A Self-Concept Approach to Teaching, Learning, and Democratic Practice*. Belmont, CA: Wadsworth Publishing Company, 1996.

—*Teaching Class Clowns (and What They Can Teach Us)*. Thousand Oaks, CA: Corwin Press, 2006.

—and John M. Novak. *Fundamentals of Invitational Education*. Kennesaw, GA: The International Alliance for Invitational Education, 2008.

—and Paula Helen Stanley. *The Inviting School Treasury: 1001 Ways to Invite School Success*. New York: Scholastic, Inc., 1994.

Roberts, Terry and the staff of the National Paideia Center. *The Power of Paideia Schools: Defining Lives Through Learning*. Alexandria, VA: The Association for Supervision and Curriculum Development, 1998.

Samalin, Nancy. *Loving Your Child Is Not Enough: Positive Discipline That Works*. New York: Penguin Books, 1987.

Sanborn, Mark. *The Fred Factor: How Passion in Your Work*

and Life Can Turn the Ordinary into the Extraordinary.
New York: Doubleday, 2004.

Smith, Dean, et al. *The Carolina Way: Leadership Lessons From a Life in Coaching.* New York: The Penguin Press, 2004.

Steele, Shelby. *The Content of Our Character: A New Vision of Race in America.* New York: Harper Perennial, 1990.

Steinem, Gloria. *Outrageous Acts and Everyday Rebellions.* New York: Owl Books, 1983.

Sullenberger, Chesley. *Highest Duty: My Search for What Really Matters.* New York: William Morris Inc., 2009.

Teaching and Learning Are Lifelong Journeys: Thoughts on the Art of Teaching and the Meaning of Education. Ed. Patricia Wayant. Boulder, CO: Blue Mountain Press, 2003.

Swindoll, Charles R. *The Grace Awakening.* Nashville: Thomas Nelson, 2006.

Tolle, Eckhart. *A New Earth: Awakening to Your Life's Purpose.* New York: Penguin Group, 2005.

Verman, David R. *Ozzie & Harriet Had a Scriptwriter: Making Tough Choices With Your Teens in the Real World.* Wheaton, IL: Tyndale House Publishers, Inc., 1996.

Vincent, Philip Fitch. *Developing Character in Students: A Primer for Teachers, Parents and Communities.* Chapel Hill, NC: New View Publications, 1994.

—*Restoring School Civility: Creating a Caring, Responsible, and Productive School.* Chapel Hill, NC: Character Development Group, Inc., 2005.

Warren, Rick. *The Purpose Driven Life: What on Earth am I Here for?* Grand Rapids, MI: Zondervan, 2002.

Watson, Tommy. *A Face of Courage, The Tommy Watson Story: How Did He Survive?* New York: Universe, Inc., 2008.

Williams, Armstrong. *Beyond Blame: How We Can Succeed by*

Breaking the Dependency Barriers. New York: Free Press, 1995.

Williams, Juan. *Enough: The Phony Leaders, Dead-End Movements, and Culture Failure that Are Undermining Black America—and What We Can Do About It.* New York: Crown Publishers, 2006.

Williams, Walter. "Three Basic Tips on How Not to be Poor." *Times-News*, Burlington, NC, 13 May, 2005.

Winfrey, Oprah, et al. *Live Your Best Life: A Treasury of Wisdom, Wit, Advice, Interviews, and Inspiration from "O," the Oprah Magazine.* Oxmoor House.

—et al. *O's Guide to Life: The Best of the Oprah Magazine (Wisdom, Wit, Advice, Interviews, and).* Oxmoor House.

Wong, Harry K and Rosemary T. Wong. *The First Days of School: How to Be an Effective Teacher.* Mountain View, CA: Harry K. Wong Publications, Inc., 1998.

Comments and Feedback From Some Participants in
Dr. Anderson's Seminars, Conferences, and Presentations*

• *Practical, doable, and effective strategies for inviting children to learn, promoting teamwork and creating a successful learning environment.* Ginger Miller, Principal

•*Proven, research-based information, focusing on the whole child and not necessarily only on test scores. I appreciate the time and research behind the theories. My staff needs to be empowered to create winners out of all students.* Pamela Chamblee, MS Principal

• *The energy and thoroughness of Lane was inspiring and captivating every second! The information was very valuable and workable. He conducted this workshop the way I think every teacher should lead, and teach their students to get the best results and motivation that promote life-long learning success.* Jackie McLean, Dropout Prevention Coordinator

• *Dr. Anderson is obviously an experienced, wise teacher who centers education on students taking the lead and responsibility for their own learning, hence success. Covered a massive amount of material, which incidentally coincides beautifully with National Board objectives.* Terry Gribble, MS Teacher

• *I liked the information packet and clarity of the presentation. I'm so impressed with the knowledge I've gained! Great job!* Sharon Hobbs, Communities In Schools Project Director

• *Dr. Anderson's philosophy is solid with wonderful, concrete examples to make it crystal clear.* Tilda Balsey, Title 1 Reading

• *Positive, motivational, and encouraging. Makes us want to do better than ever.* Janice Lail, Teacher

• *Information from Dr. Anderson was wonderful, inspiring, joyful and fun. Just make it (the presentation) longer.* Sylvia Diane Parker, Teacher

• *Loved your idea of the CARE Center. Can't wait to take it back to my school.* Kathryn Holmberg, Teacher

• *Practical and workable techniques and methods to use in school.* Lydia Davis, Counselor

• *An Educator who knows the ultimate purpose or reason for our jobs—the children. How refreshing.* Karl Slough, Teacher

• *The presenter has helped to solidify my beliefs on how to teach children and how to begin to put into practice what I truly believe will make an impact. Thank you for examples that could be used PK-12.* Alayna Gray, Assistant Principal

• *Very informative. Wonderful strategies for organization and purpose.* Roger Sowter, Teacher

• *Good practical ideas and strategies. I like the emphasis on student accountability and fairness. Great presentation, very interesting!* Amy Eason, Teacher

Dr. Lane S. Anderson

- *Dr. Anderson is a down-to-earth, caring educator-practitioner who understands school dynamics. Bravo!* Mirka Christisan, Teacher
- *Good presentation on common sense tactics combined with ideas from educational philosophies about character and ownership.* Leigh Rogers, Teacher
- *You have a phenomenal energy and effective ideas for quality education. This was an excellent presentation and I will be using this info., and would like to have you come to our school.* Catherine Mileski, Dropout Prevention Coordinator
- *Real answers to real problems. It is so nice to hear someone agree that character development through empowerment is essential!* Kim Clarke, Assistant Principal
- *[I liked] the idea that you teach the whole child, and that everyone is accountable for the success of each child.* Rachel White, Teacher
- *These are basic programs that can be incorporated in any type of school system regardless of race, income, or intelligence.* Theresa Strickland, Teacher
- *Great strategies and techniques for administrators and teachers to use in a Title I school. Awesome!* Felicia Simmons, Principal
- *Someone finally said that kids were accountable for their education. Thank you for sending me back to school feeling good about school and my way of teaching (facilitating instruction).* Cindy Tillman, Dropout Prevention Coordinator
- *Realistic ideas, doable! Should be mandated for teachers and administrators at every school.* Dr. Jean Bullock-Stevenson, Assistant Superintendent
- *I liked Dr. A's enthusiasm and passion for creating truly educated students by encouraging teaching rather than more instruction. Great ideas for CARE Center! I hope to bring an adaptation of this to my middle school discipline committee.* Johnny Walters, Teacher
- *The presentation was useful and it does not need improving. Great!!!* Dale E. Strayhorn, Principal
- *Dynamic personality. Helped me realize common sense down-to-earth practices that we should already know.* Sarah Davis, Teacher
- *Honestly, someone for the 'student.' Presentation was very knowledgeable, fun, and useful!* Lisa Clemons, Dropout Prevention Coordinator
- *Excellent information! Looking forward to using suggested techniques.* Shirley Powell, Teacher
- *Dr. A! What a blessing he was to our school. He empowered us and made us feel as if there are solutions to today's school behavior concerns! A great storyteller and full of wisdom. Dr. A has real life experiences to bring to struggling schools.* C.A. Hendrickson, Teacher

*Used with written permission from participants.